Praise for *Help Them Grow or Watch Them Go*

"Deceptively simple. Absolutely relevant. Bev and Julie demystify career development and give managers the key to unlocking the potential around them."

—**Heidi Brandow, Director, Global Learning and Development, Tesla, Inc.**

"Life and business are all about where you pay attention. Pay attention to the growth of your people . . . and they will grow your business. The authors do a great job in spelling out the how-tos!"

—**Chip Conley, author of *Wisdom@Work* and Strategic Advisor for Hospitality and Leadership, Airbnb**

"This edition takes us into the realities of today's business landscape and shows that if we want to grow our business, we have to grow our people. It walks the reader through career conversations in a way that isn't overwhelming and rather focuses on leaders being genuine and having meaningful conversations."

—**Robin Cerrati, Vice President, Human Resources, Compass Group**

"Should be the career conversation bible for busy leaders!"

—**Marshall Goldsmith, author of the *New York Times* bestseller *Triggers* and coauthor of *How Women Rise***

"Organizations in Asia need to take career development initiatives seriously, and managers need to be supported with simple skills and tools to build trust and overcome cultural barriers. This book offers an approach to career development that works cross-culturally and enables companies in Asia to deal more effectively with this talent management challenge."

—**Tan Siew Inn, Founding Partner, The Flame Centre, Singapore, and author of *Wholeness in a Disruptive World***

"*Help Them Grow or Watch Them Go* is an important contribution to leading organizations where people and talent growth matters to success."

—**Kevin Wilde, Executive Leadership Fellow, Carlson School of Management**

"In all my years coaching executives on career development, this is the best and most comprehensive resource available. It takes the complex issue of career development and simplifies it with real, action-oriented tips, tools, and insights. It's relevant for new supervisors, senior executives, and HR professionals at any level in any industry."

—**Sharon Silverman, Senior Vice President, Talent Acquisition, Gingerfinds**

"At last, a hands-on book that's smart, practical, and honest. Everyone knows that people make all the difference; this book will teach you how to make a difference with your people."

—**Alan Webber, cofounder of *Fast Company*, author of *Rules of Thumb*, and Mayor of Santa Fe, New Mexico**

"Improving the skills of our workforce is one of the country's most important economic challenges. It has to start with employers, and *Help Them Grow or Watch Them Go* tells you how to do it painlessly."
  —**Peter Cappelli, Director, Center for Human Resources, The Wharton School, and Professor of Management, University of Pennsylvania**

"Great read for those who want to help individuals develop. It is full of useful materials that are easy to access. Ideal for a manager who wants to learn about coaching others."
  —**Edward E. Lawler III, Distinguished Professor of Business, Marshall School of Business, University of Southern California, and coauthor of *Management Reset***

"Improving retention and building engagement are the driving factors for the talent development strategy of the Hearst Capital Management group. We're implementing *Help Them Grow* concepts because they provide managers and employees with an easy-to-follow yet impactful framework for career conversations. Through career conversations, we're increasing engagement and, more importantly, supporting our employees' careers."
  —**Heather Ragone, Senior Director, Talent Development, Hearst**

"Ingersoll Rand's focus on development is improving year over year. Our leaders don't just coach for performance, they coach for development. How does best-in-class engagement and employee retention sound to you? Does an organization filled with career coaches sound interesting? Read this book!"
  —**Craig Mundy, Vice President, Human Resources, Strategic Business Units, Ingersoll Rand**

"*Help Them Grow or Watch Them Go* provides a practical road map for managers who know that they want to help their teams but may not know the clear, specific steps they can take. Managers, employees, and the organizations they serve will benefit from the wisdom in this book."
  —**Rebecca L. Ray, PhD, Executive Vice President, Human Capital, The Conference Board**

"I loved this book. Draw from the abundant list of simple yet powerful questions and become the best talent manager in your organization."
  —**Tina Sung, Vice President, Government Transformation and Agency Partnerships, Partnership for Public Service**

"A great guidebook for those whose job it is to help other people grow, with all the right questions we need to be asking!"
  —**Frances Hesselbein, President and CEO, The Frances Hesselbein Leadership Institute**

Help Them **Grow** or Watch Them **Go**

Help Them Grow or Watch Them Go

CAREER **CONVERSATIONS** **ORGANIZATIONS** NEED AND **EMPLOYEES** WANT

SECOND EDITION

Beverly Kaye and Julie Winkle Giulioni

Berrett–Koehler Publishers, Inc.
a BK Business book

Berrett-Koehler Publishers, Inc.
1333 Broadway, Suite 1000
Oakland, CA 94612-1921
Tel: (510) 817-2277
Fax: (510) 817-2278
www.bkconnection.com

ORDERING INFORMATION

Quantity sales. Special discounts are available on quantity purchases by corporations, associations, and others. For details, contact the "Special Sales Department" at the Berrett-Koehler address above.

Individual sales. Berrett-Koehler publications are available through most bookstores. They can also be ordered directly from Berrett-Koehler: Tel: (800) 929-2929; Fax: (802) 864-7626; www.bk connection.com.

Orders for college textbook/course adoption use. Please contact Berrett-Koehler: Tel: (800) 929-2929; Fax: (802) 864-7626.

Distributed to the U.S. trade and internationally by Penguin Random House Publisher Services.

Berrett-Koehler and the BK logo are registered trademarks of Berrett-Koehler Publishers, Inc.

Printed in Canada

Berrett-Koehler books are printed on long-lasting acid-free paper. When it is available, we choose paper that has been manufactured by environmentally responsible processes. These may include using trees grown in sustainable forests, incorporating recycled paper, minimizing chlorine in bleaching, or recycling the energy produced at the paper mill.

Library of Congress Cataloging in Publication

Names: Kaye, Beverly, 1943–   author. | Giulioni, Julie Winkle, author.
  Title: Help them grow or watch them go : career conversations organizations need and employees want / Beverly Kaye and Julie Winkle Giulioni.
  Description: Second edition. | Oakland, CA : Berrett-Koehler Publishers, Inc., [2019] | Includes bibliographical references and index.
  Identifiers: LCCN 2018040070 | ISBN 9781523097500 (print paperpack : alk. paper)
  Subjects: LCSH: Career development.
  Classification: LCC HF5549.5.C35 K39 2019 | DDC 658.3/124--dc23
  LC record available at https://lccn.loc.gov/2018040070

27 26 25 24 23 22 21 20 19   10 9 8 7 6 5 4 3

Book produced by BookMatters, cover and text designed by Nancy Austin, copyedited by Amy Smith Bell, proofread by Janet Reed Blake, and indexed by Leonard Rosenbaum.

From Julie,

To Peter for knowing I could do this—and making sure I did.

To Nick and Jenna for the constant joy and lessons learned from watching you grow.

From Beverly,

To Barry for truly being the wind beneath my wings.

To Lindsey and Jill for showing me that I still have a lot to learn.

CONTENTS

INTRODUCTION

DEVELOPMENT DEBUNKED

Developing employees. Helping them grow. It's like eating properly or exercising.

You know it's good. You know you should. Yet, if you're like any managers today, you just don't do it as well or as frequently as you would like.

In survey after survey, year after year, employees express their dissatisfaction with how they are being supported in their careers. At the same time, managers across industries, regions, and levels uniformly report a moderate to severe lack of competence, comfort, and confidence in themselves in regards to this critical job expectation.

What IF...

▶ you could more easily and frequently engage in the career development work that employees crave without sacrificing everything else that must get done?

▶ employees assumed greater responsibility for their careers?

▶ it was possible for career development to be integrated into the work that needs to get done as opposed to being a separate series of overwhelming tasks that have to be checked off a list?

You could. They can. And it can be. That's why we've written this book.

HELP THEM gROW

In the seven years since we wrote the first edition of this book, career development has only become more important. In today's business environment, talent continues to be the major differentiator. As artificial intelligence and other advances take hold, we're coming to terms with the reality that there's no substitute for what human beings are uniquely suited to contribute to the workplace. As a result, developing people to optimize their capacity has become a compelling and strategic priority across organizations.

Developing talent is also recognized as one of the most significant drivers of employee engagement, which in turn is the key to the business outcomes you seek: revenue, profitability, innovation, productivity, customer loyalty, quality, cycle time reduction, and more—everything organizations need to survive and thrive.

But the reality of career development continues to morph in response to the evolving business landscape. Boomers are living longer—and working longer. Belt-tightening efforts that led to delayering and downsizing show no signs of loosening. There are fewer and fewer levels of management to which to aspire. Work gets organized and done more organically these days. More jobs are being filled with contingent workers. All of this breeds a sense of scarcity and leaves the impression that there aren't as many opportunities as there once were. This makes career development more important and more complex than ever before.

OR WATCH THEM *GO*

Ignore the development imperative at your own peril. Every day, employees who believe that their careers are not getting the attention they deserve make the decision to leave. Some resign to pursue employment in organizations that offer greater opportunity. Others decide the freelance life fits them better, and they cobble together a variety of projects that become their career.

But an equally dangerous group is made up of those who stay but withdraw their engagement, motivation, and enthusiasm for the work.

And all of this matters. A lot. Economic researchers point to evolving skill gaps, changes to immigration policies, and changing demographics as indicators that we are in for a sustained labor shortage. Cities—looking to build their populations—are considering paying people to relocate. Buckle up. It's going to be a bumpy ride: retention—if it's not already—is going to keep managers awake at night.

THE "THEM" IN *HELP THEM GROW*: WHO ARE THEY?

When we wrote the first edition of this book in 2012, we loosely used the word *employee* to refer to the bulk of the people who work for you. Ah, what a difference a few years can make. Today, full-time employees make up just over half of the workforce. The rest is comprised of part-time employees, contractors, consultants, interns, and more. Gig workers are a significant economic and employment factor.

As the number of these nontraditional contributors grows, organizations and managers grapple with hard questions around effectiveness and equity. Let us offer a simple and proactive solution: Develop them all! It's time to take a more generous and democratic approach to growth. We know what you're thinking:

▶ Yes, gig workers may not be with you for long.

▶ Yes, the contingent workforce will build skills that they may pack up and take elsewhere.

▶ Yes, the same is true of your full-timers.

No longer are there lifetime employment guarantees or gold watches. You know it and so does your workforce. Today they're looking for other sources of security—skills, knowledge, and experiences. Offer these and—although there's no guarantee that people will stay longer—

they'll be able to contribute more while they're with you. And you'll build an attractive employment brand in a competitive marketplace.

We'll still use the word *employee* throughout this book, but we strongly suggest that you read it as *everybody* and apply these ideas to the full range of people—regardless of employment status—with whom you work.

CAREER CONVERSATIONS ORGANIZATIONS NEED AND EMPLOYEES WANT

So what's a manager to do? Plenty. And it might be easier than you expect.

Quality Career Development

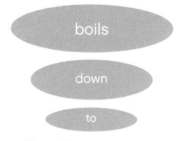

Quality Conversations

Quality career development boils down to quality conversations.

Throughout this book, we'll challenge you to reframe career development in such a way that responsibility rests squarely with the employee, and that your role becomes more about prompting, guiding, reflecting, exploring ideas, activating enthusiasm, and driving action. This role centers around talking about rather than actually doing the heavy lifting of development.

We'll offer a framework for thinking about conversations that help others grow. It involves three distinct types of conversations: hindsight, foresight, and insight.

▶ Hindsight conversations help others look backward and inward to determine who they are, where they've been, what they love, and where they excel. Chapters 3 and 4 provide questions and ideas for helping others look back as a basis for moving forward.

▶ Foresight conversations are designed to keep employees looking forward and outward toward changes, trends, and the ever-evolving big picture. Chapter 5 offers easy, straightforward tools that are long on value and short on your time investment.

▶ Leveraging the insights that surface from the convergence of hindsight and foresight is the focus of Chapters 6, 7, and 8. How do the employee's strengths fit into where the organization or industry is going? Where are there opportunities to carve out a space to grow and perform? How can we help others update their definitions of career success? Of the work that needs to be done, which activities will give people unique experiences and fodder for development?

▶ But how can you make all of this happen at the speed of business? Chapter 9 outlines how to grow with the flow or embed development into everyday life through heightened awareness and fluid conversation strategies.

▶ In Chapter 10 we'll wrap up with a discussion of the kind of culture that supports authentic, sustainable career development.

HOW TO READ THIS BOOK

You're probably doing a pretty good job so far. Here are a few thoughts to get the most from the experience.

This book was written for anyone who has a role in developing others. The titles vary from organization to organization: supervisor, manager, director, team lead, vice president, CEO. Seasoned executives to first-time frontline leaders. Line and staff personnel. For-profit and nonprofit leaders. Small business owners. Readers have told us that the ideas we share apply equally well at home to the very human domain of parenting and even life in general.

We've chosen to use the term *manager* generically. Whenever you see it, *manager* means you.

This book is all about the career conversations employees want. So we'll draw heavily upon the employee's voice. These are real individuals in the workplace whose eloquent insights make the point far better than we could. They aren't the entitled whiners with unrealistic expectations. They're your solid citizens. The ones you count on to produce. The ones you're hoping will stick around.

► TRY THIS

You'll find lots of questions and activities you can use with your employees. We'll call them out like this. Have an upcoming career conversation? Scan the pages for an exercise, tuck the book under your arm, and you're ready to go.

WHAT ABOUT YOU?

So you're somebody's employee too, right? And, if you're like many managers, you get caught in the middle, doing the right thing for your employees, but not necessarily having it done for you. As you read this book, you may find yourself thinking, *This sounds pretty good, but what about me?* Answer: do it yourself!

The tools and questions throughout this book are highly flexible. Change *you* to *I* and you're ready for some self-discovery. You might find it helpful to review the answers with someone at work or at home. A fresh set of eyes may pick up clues and offer a different perspective and new insights. Bottom line: as you invest in building skills to support your employees' development, don't be afraid to be selfish and apply what you're learning to yourself and your own career as well.

We'll close each chapter with some what-ifs. We know that as a manager responsible for delivering business results, you must keep your feet planted firmly on the ground. So, from that grounded position, take a moment to consider what just might be possible.

What IF...

▶ you kept reading and tried out even one or two ideas with your employees?

. . . .

They would *grow*.

1

Develop Me
OR I'm
History!

Spending forty-sixty-eighty hours somewhere each week…I want it to mean something. I want to feel like I'm moving forward somehow. If I can't grow here, I've gotta look elsewhere.

—An employee (perhaps yours)

The decision to assume a management role in today's workplace comes with a front-row seat to some of the greatest business challenges of our time. Day in and day out, you must

Do more with less. It's become cliché, but it permeates life at work. You've likely become a master at finding ways to reduce costs, time, and other resources below levels you ever imagined were possible.

Navigate unprecedented uncertainty and complexity. The unknowns outnumber the knowns today. Yet others look to you for clarity and direction in an increasingly unpredictable environment.

Meet ever-expanding expectations. Every quarter, you're asked to do a little (or a lot) more. Bigger sales. Greater numbers of service interactions. More projects. Higher scores.

Continuously improve quality. Good enough isn't. Given the competition in today's global market, perfection is the standard—until it's met and you have to do even better.

Deliver the next big thing. Most organizations believe that if they're not moving forward, they're sliding backward. Innovation gets its picture on business magazine covers because it represents the promise of greater success.

And, no matter how long, hard, or smart you work, you can't do all of this alone. Success depends upon tapping the very best that everyone has to offer. (By *everyone*, we're not just talking about employees—because the workforce has dramatically grown to include gig workers, contingent support, contractors and consultants, interns and even

Career development is among the **most** frequently **forgotten tools** for driving business results... yet it's **completely within** a **manager's** sphere of **influence**.

externs.) So today, your success rests upon finding ways to continuously expand everyone's capacity, engagement, and ability to contribute to the organization.

Study after study confirms that best-in-class managers—those who consistently develop the most capable, flexible, and engaged teams able to drive exceptional business results—all share one quality: they make career development a priority.

A "HISTORY" LESSON

Even during challenging economic times, your best and brightest have options. Failing to help them grow can lead employees to take their talents elsewhere. They become "history." But what can be equally damaging as this talent drain are the employees who stay and become disengaged. Their bodies show up for work every day but their commitment has quit.

So, if career development is a tool that can deliver what organizations need most—productivity gains, expense reduction, retention, quality improvements, innovation, and bottom-line results—why isn't everyone using it?

DEFINING TERMS

Perhaps it's frequently forgotten because the term *career development* strikes fear into managers' hearts.

WHAT ABOUT YOU?

Take a moment to think about what *career development* means to you? What's involved? What's your role?

Whatever your answer, we'll bet that ours is simpler. You see, many managers are intimidated by or steer clear of career development because they have a mistaken, outdated, or overwhelming definition of the term.

So try this definition on for size:

Career development
is nothing more than
helping others grow.
And nothing less.

Helping others grow can take a nearly unlimited number of forms. On one end of the continuum, you help employees prepare for and move to new or expanded roles in obvious and visible ways. But far more frequently, growth shows up on the other end of the continuum, in small, subtle ways that quietly create greater challenge, interest, and satisfaction in a job.

The problem is that too often, career development evokes images of forms, checklists, and deadlines. And let's be honest—the organization needs you to comply with these processes and systems to support important human resources planning work. But administrative details are not career development. Unfortunately, these artifacts too frequently overshadow the true art of development.

Genuine, meaningful, and sustainable career development occurs through the human act of conversation.

Whether it's a formal individual development planning (IDP) meeting or an on-the-fly connection, it's the quality of the conversation that matters most to employees. That's how they judge your performance and their development. That's also how they make the decision to go or stay—or to stay and disengage.

So, if it really is as simple as just talking to people, why isn't career development a more common feature of the organizational landscape?

Careers
are
developed
one
conversation
at a **time...**
over time.

IMMOBILIZING MYTHS

Over the years, managers—by sharing oral history and spinning lore—have created and continue to propagate several myths. And these myths (read: reasons or excuses) keep them from having the very career conversations their employees want. Which are familiar to you?

Myth 1 — There is simply not enough time.

No one will argue that time is among the scarcest resources available to managers today. But let's get real. You're having conversations already—probably all day long. What if you could redirect some of that time and some of those conversations to focus on careers?

Myth 2 — If I don't talk about it, they may not think about it and the status quo will be safe.

Why invite problems? Developing people could lead them to leave and upset the balance of your well-running department, right? Wrong. Employees have growth on their minds—whether you address it or not. Withholding these conversations is a greater danger to the status quo than engaging in them.

Myth 3 — Since employees need to own their careers, it's not my job.

No one will argue that managers own the development of their employees' careers. Employees do. But that doesn't mean that managers are completely off the hook. You have an essential role in helping and supporting others to take responsibility. And that role plays out in large part through conversation.

Myth 4 — Everyone wants more, bigger, or better: promotions, raises, prestige, power.

If you believe this one, you likely view career development as a confounding no-win situation. Because these things you imagine others want are in woefully short supply, it's understandable that many managers would avoid a potentially disappointing and demoralizing conversation. But based on our research, the fundamental assumption behind this response is patently inaccurate. When asked about what they want to get out of a career conversation with their managers, the number-one response from employees is "ways to use my talents creatively."

Myth 5 — Development efforts are best concentrated on high potentials, many of whom already have plans in place.

This one's a cop-out. You can indeed see a significant return on the development you invest in your high potentials. But they make up only about 10 percent of your population—maybe less. You probably have another 10 percent of marginal performers who are on a very different kind of plan—hopefully fewer. But what about the 80 percent in between—the massive middle responsible for doing the bulk of the work? Imagine what even a small investment in their development might yield.

If you're like most managers, a few of these myths likely make sense to you. Dog-ear or bookmark this page and come back to it after you've completed the book. We predict that when you are introduced to a different way of looking at your role, you may also look at career development and these myths a little differently.

But, until then, remember this: growing the business means growing people. Forget that—and the rest is history.

What IF...

▶ you reframed how you think about career development?

▶ growth really was as simple as conversing with employees?

▶ managers could break through the myths that undermine their success and their employees' growth?

2

Can We Talk?

I'm realistic. I know your time is tight and that you've got lots of other priorities. My career probably isn't at the top of your list. Don't worry—I've gotten the message that I own my career. I just need a thinking partner who'll help me step back every once in a while and focus on my development.

—An employee (perhaps yours)

If you're like most managers, you care. You've become accustomed to taking on more and more, expanding your job description with countless "other duties as assigned"—and even some that aren't. Developing the careers of the people who report to you is on a growing (read: crushing) list of to-dos.

What if you could reimagine your role around helping others grow? What if you reframed this task (which, let's face it, gets put on the back burner most of the time anyway) in such a way that responsibility rests squarely with the employee? What if your role was more about prompting, guiding, reflecting, exploring ideas, activating enthusiasm, and driving action rather than actually doing all the work?

Guess what? That's how it should be. And that's how you help people take responsibility for their careers. That's also how you can fit career development into your already full day.

Somehow the simple human act of helping people grow has gotten very complicated—processes on top of checklists with references to resource guides—and the to-do list keeps growing. Is it any wonder that you want to steer clear?

But managers who do this well cut through the clutter and have figured out what employees really need. And it's much more basic than you might imagine.

"I got tired of orchestrating these development experiences for people who just blew them off like they were nothing. I finally saw that the gift of heavy lifting I was giving my people was not appreciated. If I owned their development plans, they didn't. So I backed way off. Now, I'm totally there for them, will talk it all out, explore possibilities, help them think it through. But, when it comes to making it happen, they've got to take the lead. That's their job.**"**

—Manager, logistics

For years we've heard that talk is cheap. Not true.

Astute managers have gotten comfortable with talking more and doing less. These are no slugs—they're strategists. They appreciate the power of conversations to inspire and generate change in others.

Conversation has the power to touch employees' hearts and minds more deeply than the well-intentioned steps you might take on their behalf. You need nothing more than your own words to inspire reflection and commitment. From that can spring employee-generated actions, actions that employees own, actions that will help them realize their personal definitions of success.

Career development is all about the conversation.

"The action is in the interaction.**"**

—Douglas Conant, former Campbell Soup CEO
and author of *Touchpoints*

Genuine career development is not about forms, choreographing new assignments, or orchestrating promotions. It's about the quality of the conversations between a manager and an employee, conversations that are designed to

▶ Facilitate insights and awareness

▶ Explore possibilities and opportunities

▶ Inspire responses that drive employee-owned action

When it comes to the **manager's role** in development, **talk** is **actually the most precious** and results-driving commodity you have to **share**.

ONE AND DONE IS DONE

Responding to the ever-quickening pace of business, many organizations are rethinking a variety of time-honored (and time-consuming) practices. For instance, performance appraisals, once the centerpiece of management, are being eliminated or reconstituted in very different ways.

So what about career development? If you're like the vast majority of managers expected to operate at the speed of business, you may no longer feel that you have the luxury of annual or semiannual career dialogues.

And that's not a problem—it's actually an opportunity. Because you don't have to hold lengthy summits with employees, solving all of the career problems of the world in one big meeting to help others get results. In fact, in many cases less can be more.

"After a few years, I realized what the annual development process reminded me of—New Year's resolutions! It was energizing to set out the plan, and we paid attention to it for a while. But pretty soon, it was tucked away until the following year when we'd smile at our folly and rededicate ourselves to a new batch."

—Marketing director

When you reframe *career development* in terms of ongoing conversations—rather than procedural checkpoints or scheduled activities—suddenly you have more flexibility and the chance to develop careers organically, when and where authentic opportunities arise.

LESS IS MORE

An interaction doesn't require a minimum threshold to count as a conversation. You don't get more points for length. You get more points for stimulating thinking.

Would you rather...

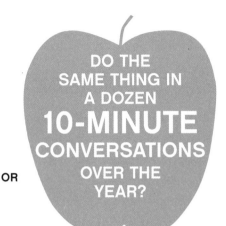

Note: Do the math. It's the same 120 minutes just offered up in smaller, bite-size servings.

Increasingly, organizations and the time-starved managers within them are opting for shorter, more frequent conversations that can cover the same ground as their heftier cousins (maybe more) but in an iterative and ongoing fashion. The benefits are compelling:

► Shorter conversations fit better with the cadence of business today.

► Frequent, ongoing dialogue communicates a genuine commitment to the employee and development.

► Iterative conversations allow employees to layer awareness, insights, and action more naturally.

► The ongoing nature of the conversation keeps development alive in everyone's mind (as opposed to tucking it away for a formal meeting).

► These frequent exchanges sustain momentum, fuel progress, and act as an ongoing reminder of the organization's commitment to employee learning, growth, and progress.

Some call it *embedded*. Others *on-the-fly* or *in-the-moment*. We call it a contemporary solution to a perennial problem. Short, targeted, ongoing career conversations are efficient—for you and the employee—

because they happen within the workflow where genuine opportunities exist.

BECOME UNBALANCED

Think about the most interesting and engaging conversations you've experienced. Either you got to do most of the talking or the dialogue moved fluidly back and forth, allowing everyone to share airtime evenly. Now, forget all that.

A career conversation is completely unbalanced in favor of your employees. If you do your job well, they will be doing 90 percent of the talking. If you're talking more than the remaining 10 percent, you're likely taking on too much responsibility for employees' development and robbing them of ownership for their careers.

Striking this unbalance requires a particular skill on the part of the manager: asking quality questions.

> **" My first real manager had this way of asking these questions that wormed their way into my brain and ultimately demanded answers."**
>
> —Supervisor, finance and accounting

If the work of career development happens within the context of conversation, the primary tool of the trade must be the question.

Thoughtfully conceived and well-timed questions make things happen. They

► Provoke reflection, constructive discomfort, insight, ideas, and action in others

► Keep the focus squarely on the employee

► Demonstrate that you respect and value the other person

► Reinforce the shift of ownership for development to the employee

We are so sold on the value of questions, that we've included one hundred throughout this book.

You **don't**
have to have
all the
answers.

But,
what's **not negotiable**
is that you
have the
questions.

? ? ? ? ? ? ? ? ? ?

CULTIVATING CURIOSITY

Questions are a powerful tool. Add the spirit of curiosity, and you've got an unbeatable combination.

But, let's face it—curiosity doesn't come quite as naturally or easily to us as adults as it did when we were kids.

Blame it on time scarcity or information overload or our search-engine culture that reinforces a laserlike focus on what we think we want to know.

Whatever is to blame, there's a powerful case for overcoming it, because curiosity is not just informative—it's also transformative.

People recognize and respond deeply to genuine curiosity on the part of their leaders. It leaves them feeling cared for, valued, validated, and like they matter—all of which fuels stronger relationships, retention, and results.

Take the quiz on the next page to evaluate your level of curiosity.

If you answered "no" to four or more of the questions, you have an opportunity to cultivate greater curiosity. But you're likely an over-achiever and realize that even one "no" offers a chance for improvement.

Curiosity might be the most under-the-radar and undervalued leadership competency in business today. Think about it: What could you accomplish if you practiced passionate listening—really listening with intention and a true sense of purpose to learn and understand? What possibilities could you cultivate if you honed your ability to wonder out loud with those around you? What innovations and breakthroughs might you spark if you could bring new eyes and genuine inquisitiveness to old relationships and problems?

Developing the ability to approach individuals, situations, and conversations with curiosity can affect your own energy and enthusiasm, relationships with others, and hard business results—not to mention the quality of your career conversations.

WHAT ABOUT YOU? ·····················

You might be able to fake listening, but not curiosity. Test your own Curiosity Quotient (CQ).

I am comfortable entering a conversation not knowing how it will turn out.	❐ YES	❐ NO
I can suspend judgment and skepticism.	❐ YES	❐ NO
I expect to be surprised when I talk with others.	❐ YES	❐ NO
I can suspend my need to fix situations and solve problems.	❐ YES	❐ NO
I am sincerely interested in what most people have to say.	❐ YES	❐ NO
I believe that there's no shame in admitting I don't understand something.	❐ YES	❐ NO
I ask questions without having a "right" answer in mind.	❐ YES	❐ NO
I am energized by finding out what makes others tick.	❐ YES	❐ NO
I am motivated to dig deeper when I sense hesitancy or want to learn more.	❐ YES	❐ NO
I enjoy learning things about people that I didn't know before.	❐ YES	❐ NO
I am comfortable following someone else's lead in a conversation.	❐ YES	❐ NO
I believe that people are interesting and complex.	❐ YES	❐ NO

HIGH-IMPACT PRACTICES

Four high-impact practices can help cultivate and bring greater curiosity to your interactions with others.

Lose control.

Curiosity is all about becoming comfortable with what's not known. Successful and curious managers know that this means consciously entering a conversation not knowing how it will turn out and asking questions you don't know the answers to. It means not guiding others toward the *right* answers you have in mind. It frequently means following someone else's conversational lead rather than your own. Curiosity means taking a leap of faith, letting go of the need to control, and trusting that all will unfold—perhaps even better than if you continue to force it.

Jettison judgment.

Be honest. How many words does someone speak before you've decided who they are, what they're like, or what they're trying to communicate? There's an epidemic of judgment and skepticism in the workplace. Perhaps it's because of time pressures. Perhaps it's due to confidence that our instincts will guide us. The reason matters less than this: curiosity and judgment cannot coexist. The most successful and curious managers have developed the ability to suspend judgment. They engage fully without the need to put people or issues in tidy boxes. They appreciate the value of getting the whole story—especially when it comes to development.

GAG your "fix it" reflex.

You've risen to your management role because you're good at solving problems. Yet overused, this skill can at the least endanger (and in some cases completely extinguish) curiosity. It's all too common for a manager to volunteer a resolution or generate elements of a development plan—all with the best of intentions. But engaging the other person promotes greater growth and allows managers to learn more in the process.

WOO the cue.

Successful, curious managers are not passive "consumers" of information. They engage actively with others. They are on high alert for signals and cues that require exploration. An emotionally charged word. A facial expression. A pause or hesitance. A reaction. All are invitations to dig deeper, follow up, ask for examples, or just invite the other person to say more. These cues are like traffic signs, helping managers navigate the career conversation with curiosity and purpose.

Quality questions asked *without* curiosity will signal to employees that you've just come back from training.

Quality questions asked *with* the spirit of curiosity will facilitate conversations that will allow others to literally change their lives.

CLOSURE IS OVERRATED

Given this focus on asking questions, it bears repeating that you don't have to have all the answers. Neither does the employee, for that matter. In fact, not having all the answers may actually drive more thought and energy.

According to Russian psychologist Bluma Zeigarnik (in "The Retention of Completed and Uncompleted Actions," which appeared in *Psychological Research* in 1927), we remember better what's incomplete. The problem is that this lack of closure generates an internal tension for many. The mind, uncomfortable with what has been left unfinished, continues to focus on the question or problem.

So what does this science have to do with helping your people grow? Many managers shy away from hard questions and conversations where they might not have all the answers. If you're one of them, you don't have to do that any longer. Quite the opposite. Go ahead and courageously ask the challenging questions and even end the conversation with a real tough or thought-provoking one that the employee can contemplate for a while.

Don't feel the pressure to wrap up every conversation with a bow. Closure is overrated. Unfinished business . . . that's what will cause employees to continue to ponder and will ultimately spark action and feed progress.

Closure is overrated.

Unfinished business . . .

that's what will cause employees to continue to ponder and will ultimately

✳**spark**✳ **action**

and **feed progress.**

► TRY THIS: OPEN-ENDED
. . . .

End your next meeting or conversation with a question. Explain that there's
no time for a discussion, but that you've been thinking about it. The next
time you are with that person or those people, ask if anyone remembers
the question. You'll be surprised that not only do they remember the question, they'll also have quite a few answers for you.

HINDSIGHT, FORESIGHT, INSIGHT

So what are all these unbalanced, curious, unfinished conversations
supposed to be about? More than you might expect. Too frequently we
limit the scope of career conversations, thinking they're only about
jobs, promotions, or stretch assignments—the actions employees can
take to move forward. Important? Yes. But that's just a drop in the
bucket of conversations you can have with employees.

Whether your conversations are more formal and lengthy or shorter
and iterative, helping others pursue their career goals involves facilitating an exploration of three key areas: hindsight, foresight, and insight.

HINDSIGHT   **FORESIGHT**

                    INSIGHT

Framing the Conversations

Hindsight. This is a look backward to develop a deep understanding of such things as where employees have been, what they love, and what they're good at. Self-perception is key; and it becomes even clearer when enhanced (and sometimes moderated) by feedback from others. This backward glance—on the part of the employee and those around them—is essential for moving forward.

Foresight. This involves a bigger-picture look at the broader environment and the business in order to determine what's changing and what those changes mean for the future. Since nobody wants to pursue a career direction for which no need exists, foresight is critical.

Insight. This is the sweet spot where hindsight (where you've been and what you want to be doing) converges with foresight (organizational needs and opportunities). It's where you jointly determine with the employee the full range of ways to move forward and the actions to take to achieve career objectives.

This is not an academic model cooked up in a social science lab. It's a framework (based on more than forty years of working with real people and their real challenges) that flexes to address the many types of career conversations available to managers. This framework operates and supports you on three different levels.

Micro — You can ask a question from any of the three areas to informally spark reflection and interest.

Macro — You can blend the three areas into one short conversation that can occur spontaneously in the workflow to help employees advance their career thinking.

Mega — You can apply this framework and the questions associated with hindsight, foresight, and insight to your organization's formal individual development planning (IDP) process for richer results.

The following chapters delve into hindsight, foresight, and insight and how you can use them to keep employees satisfied, engaged, and always growing.

What IF . . .

► employees really owned their own careers?

► your job was to facilitate conversations rich with insightful questions that would guide others toward greater awareness and action?

► these conversations were shorter, more frequent, and occurred within the natural flow of the work?

► you didn't pressure yourself to have all the answers?

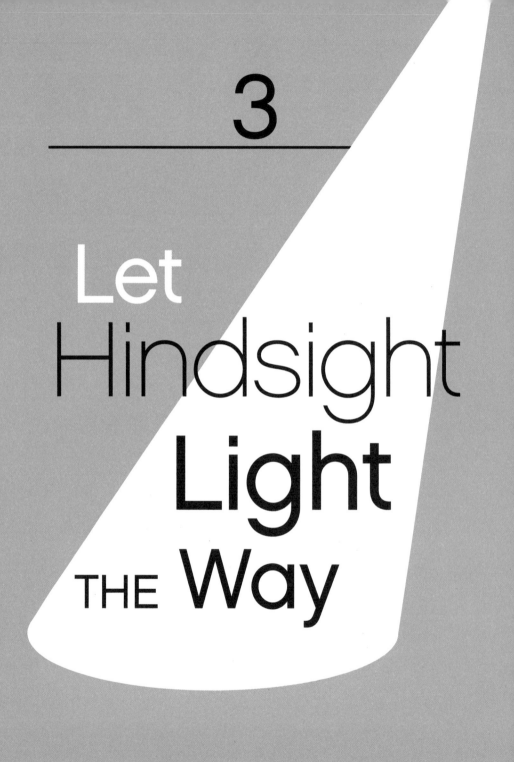

3

Let Hindsight Light THE Way

My interview for this job was so great. The manager was really interested in learning about my background and how I'd applied myself in the past. He asked great, probing questions that really challenged me to think. I sure wish he would "interview" me like that again now that I've got the job.

—An employee (perhaps yours)

Imagine if the job interview was the beginning of an ongoing conversational thread throughout someone's career. Imagine uncovering layer upon layer of your employees' skills, abilities, interests, and more—right up to the day they retire. Imagine what you could do with that information. Imagine what the employee could do with it.

Your employees' ability to take satisfying and productive steps toward career goals is directly proportionate to their self-awareness.

LOOKING BACK TO MOVE FORWARD

You can enable career-advancing self-awareness by helping employees take stock of where they've been, what they've done, and who they are. Looking back thoughtfully is what hindsight conversations are all about. They surface what people need to know and understand about themselves to approach future career steps in a productive and satisfying way.

For hindsight to be as clear as possible, though, two different perspectives are required. The employee's self-perception is the starting point. (That's what this chapter is all about.) But it needs to be confirmed, challenged, enhanced, and otherwise worked over with information gathered from others. When employees, coworkers, and you (the manager) also look back at performance and results, hindsight gets that much closer to 20/20. (Just wait until the next chapter for more about feedback.)

Hindsight allows employees to develop a clear view of their

▶ Skills and strengths—what they're good at

▶ Values—what's most important

▶ Interests—what keeps them engaged

▶ Dislikes—what they want to steer clear of

▶ Preferences—how they like to work

▶ Weaknesses—what they struggle with

Clarity around these factors allows for intentional movement toward career objectives. Otherwise, people may engage in lots of activity that's not focused or that takes them in directions that aren't consistent with who they are and what they really want to do.

❝I worked for years to get that senior troubleshooter promotion. Put everything into it. But when I got it, I was miserable. The travel took me away from my family for weeks on end and the work itself was really unsatisfying. I'd swoop in, do my part, and then swoop out—never seeing the end product or really feeling a part of it. If I'd really thought about it, I would have known that it wasn't a good fit. I've always been happiest being part of an ongoing team and having something tangible to show for my efforts at the end of the day.❞

—IT consultant

Hindsight conversations are the foundation of career development. They are designed to spark thinking, encourage connections, and promote discovery. They provide invaluable information to the employee and to you, the manager. You can facilitate this type of self-awareness through quality questions that

▶ Haunt the employee, popping out around every corner

▶ Percolate throughout the day—and maybe at night

▶ Worm their way around employees' minds, encouraging new areas to explore

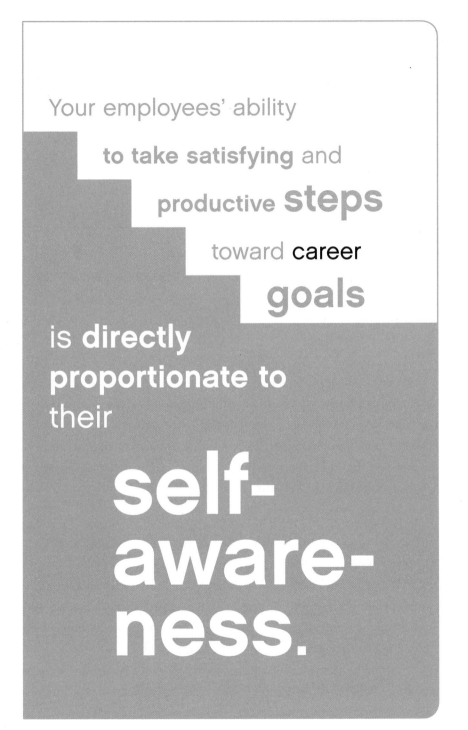

Your employees' ability to take satisfying and productive **steps** toward **career** **goals** is **directly proportionate to** their **self-aware-ness.**

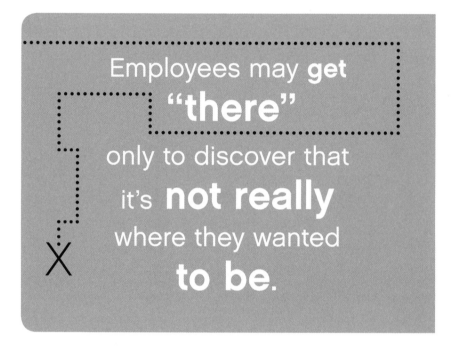

Employees may **get** "there" only to discover that it's **not really** where they wanted **to be.**

(If you're still waiting for the other shoe to drop and for us to tell you about the ten to twenty hours of additional to-dos that are required to appropriately support your employees in their career development, let it go. It's not going to happen. We're serious. You can be highly effective by just guiding the conversation. You don't have to have the answers, and you don't have to drive the action. Really!)

THE GRAVITATIONAL PULL OF WEAKNESSES

Despite considerable research and literature on the benefits of focusing on strengths, most people are more strongly drawn toward and familiar with their weaknesses. When you have a minute (literally sixty seconds), make a list of all of your strengths and weaknesses. Chances are you'll have more weaknesses than strengths on your list.

In fact, in workshop after workshop we witness a surprising human dynamic. When people are asked to create a list of their weaknesses, they do so effortlessly, smiling and sometimes laughing at the task. Ask these same people to list their strengths and you see a very different response. Furrowed brows. Head scratching. Grimaces and genuine agitation. Odd, huh?

> **WHAT ABOUT YOU?**
> You can even skip the writing and count up your strengths on one hand and weaknesses on the other. More smiles or frowns?

So employees need your help in identifying and focusing on what they do well—their talents and their gifts. These are important inputs to career decisions that frequently get lost in our weakness-centric world.

But strengths can be a little sneaky—and employees should be aware of two lesser-known laws that govern them.

Law 1 — Too much of a good thing isn't always a good thing.
A strength used to excess can actually become a problem.

When it's just right	When it's overdone
"He's organized and meets deadlines no matter what."	"You mean old steamroller?"
"Her flexible thinking really helps everyone get outside the box."	"Our weekly meetings are a total waste of time because of her lack of structure."
"He's a great negotiator."	"It wouldn't hurt him to compromise once in a while."

Strengths have a dark side. Getting in touch with the implications of too-much-of-a-good-thing helps to enhance one's self-understanding—and ultimately effectiveness.

Law 2 — Strengths are context sensitive. A strength in one setting can actually work against you in other settings. (Remember when you were first promoted into leadership? Did your strength around getting the work done ever get in the way of delegating or developing others?)

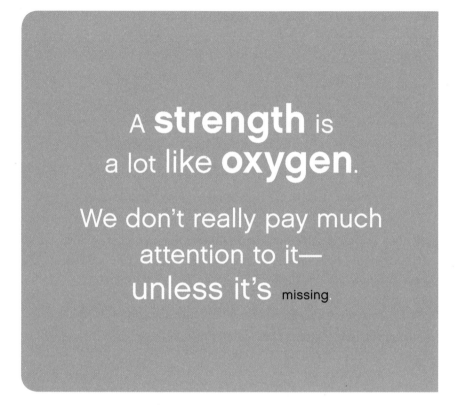

A **strength** is a lot like **oxygen**. We don't really pay much attention to it—unless it's missing.

With all this talk of strengths, let's not lose sight of the importance of understanding weaknesses, where behavior or performance could compromise the employee's career goals. Because when it comes to helping people grow and pursue career goals, a balanced view of what's working for and against you provides the strongest foundation for results.

Hindsight conversations don't need to be long or take a lot of planning time. Here are three approaches that you can prepare for in two minutes and conduct in as little as five- to ten-minute chunks around the other work that needs to get done. Choose any or all depending upon your level of comfort and the nature of the relationship you have with your employees.

► TRY THIS: GET TO KNOW THEM BACKWARD

Schedule a conversation to deliberately review an employee's past experiences, jobs, positions, and tasks to find themes, trends, and insights.

1. Start by explaining that a solid career future is based upon an understanding of who you are and what got you to where you are.

2. With the employee, create a list of the various positions, roles, and jobs they have held.

3. For each position, role, or job, ask the following questions:

   ► Which parts brought you joy, energy, and a sense of persistence?

   ► Which parts led to boredom, disengagement, and a sense of just going through the motions?

4. Step back with the employee and see what themes emerge. You won't need a PhD or psychoanalysis couch to make connections. Using questions like these will help:

   ► What thoughts/ideas repeated?

   ► How might your interests, values, and skills have evolved over time?

   ► What will you definitely want to seek out in the future?

   ► What will you definitely want to avoid in the future?

It's that straightforward. You ask the questions. They answer. And together you make sense out of it.

► TRY THIS: QUARTERLY CHECKUP

A variation of the Get-to-Know-Them-Backward theme is to close out every quarter with brief employee checkups or check-ins. The purpose of these conversations is not to evaluate business results, review sales, or negotiate productivity standards for the next quarter. Rather, the goal is to diagnose what's going on in the employee's heart and head.

Put performance entirely aside and ask questions like these:

► What was the best part of the quarter for you?

► What work did you find most satisfying?

► How often were you stretched, and how did that feel?

► At what points did you feel your energy and engagement lagging?

Make this a habit, and at least four times each year you'll help employees turn their day-to-day experiences into profound self-awareness that can inform career decisions—and a lot more.

► TRY THIS: THE NEVER-ENDING INTERVIEW

Keep the interview going by engaging in routine conversations that reveal an ever-evolving, complex, and multidimensional picture to the employee of what will be important to consider as a basis for career growth.

1. Just pull one or more questions that interest you and the employee most from the list that follows. Use them in any order. Take notes.

Skills and Strengths

► What have you always been naturally good at?

► What can't you keep yourself from doing?

► What are you known for?

Values

► Looking back, what's always been most important to you in life and in work?

► What issues or problems do you feel most strongly about?

► What are your top three values or things you hold most dear?

Interests

► What do you enjoy learning about most?

► What do you wish you had more time for?

► How would you spend your time if you didn't have to work?

Dislikes

► What kind of work have you typically gravitated away from?

► What tasks routinely get pushed to the bottom of your to-do list?

► What bores you?

Preferences

► What aspects of past jobs have you loved most?

► How do you like to work?

► What kinds of work settings/spaces help you do your best work?

Weaknesses/Opportunities

► What lessons do you find yourself learning over and over again?

► How do your strengths sometimes work against you?

► What skills do you appreciate in others that you don't always see in yourself?

2. Together determine what conclusions can be drawn by asking questions such as these:

► How do these pieces fall together?

► What picture/image does it yield?

► What are the commonalities, themes, or connection points?

Skills, strengths, values, interests, dislikes, preferences, and weaknesses converge in unique ways for each individual—like snowflakes or fingerprints.

As understanding about these things grows, people start to see an image appear that becomes a clearer picture of their lives and who they are.

But this awareness cannot be just contained to career matters. Greater personal insight can't help but spill over into day-to-day work, improving relationships, performance, and results. It starts to seep out into one's personal life—enhancing that as well. Hindsight conversations are good for the whole person—not just for the part people bring to work.

Don't be fooled. These approaches are simple, straightforward, and relatively quick. But they pack a punch. In fact, they deliver value far beyond their modest appearances.

A CASE IN POINT

"I was born to teach. It was pretty obvious from the way I was frequently the first to figure out new processes and applications and teach them to the rest of the group. My earliest memory was of getting in trouble when I (proudly) taught a fellow kindergartner how to write the first letter of her name—on the carpet. Over the years, I've found my greatest satisfaction to be in roles where I connect with and help others learn and grow. I really appreciate my manager recognizing that and encouraging me to explore opportunities in training."

—Technical trainer

COUNTERPOINT

"It's easy to pigeonhole people. Figure out what they're good at and forget the rest. Take Pat, the rock star we hired away from a competitor to manage our challenging clients. Over the years, she seemed happy doing what she was doing. Once or twice we upgraded her title and we raised her salary regularly. After all that, she resigned to take a sales job. It turns out that she had felt bored for years—was tired of what she was doing. If it had occurred to me to look past the one skill set that we myopically capitalized on, she'd still be with us today—bringing in much needed new business."

—Director, Commercial Lines Insurance

Fundamentally people want to know themselves and be known by others. Hindsight conversations satisfy that deep human need.

But helping people look back and inward also provides a reservoir of information that allows employees to move forward and toward their career goals in intentional ways that will produce satisfying results.

What IF . . .

► a little time was spent looking back before leaping forward?

► managers had the questions to help unlock what's unique within and important to each employee?

► you applied the curiosity you bring to first interviews to ongoing conversations with employees throughout their careers?

4

Feed Me

Where do I stand? How am I seen? What do you think? I don't mean to sound needy—but a little bit of information could go a long way with me.

—An employee (perhaps yours)

Feedback. How appropriate that the word begins with *feed*. Because for many employees, information from others about how they're perceived and how they're doing is a severe source of malnourishment in today's workplace.

Yet in study after study, employees in every sector are starving for feedback. This is a pretty human response. We spend more than forty hours each week at work, dedicating our bodies, minds, and souls to the cause. A little attention is not too much to ask.

Managers, beware: a low-feedback diet may be harmful to the health of your business. Side effects include

Disengagement Stunted growth
Lack of clarity Lost opportunities
Loss of talent

Good people move on—either psychologically or physically—when their hunger for feedback isn't satisfied. And this loss of talent is completely unnecessary because feedback

▶ Costs nothing except a little genuine attention to others

▶ Lends itself to literally any setting—face-to-face or virtually

▶ Requires as little as a minute of your time

▶ Extends far beyond the domain of managers—anyone who is willing or asked can get involved

Feedback is a hindsight lens through which people can pass their self-perceptions—and in the process, it yields a clearer vision of who they are and the value they bring. Effective feedback planted in a receptive mind can fuel powerful learning, exploration, challenge, and growth.

WHAT ABOUT YOU?

Be honest. When it comes to giving and getting feedback, where do you stand?

May I please make an appointment for a root canal?	No dessert for me, I'll have feedback instead!

1   10

IT'S FEEDING TIME

Opportunities for feedback abound. And what probably comes to your mind first is performance feedback—job-related information about an employee's behavior or results that helps to drive improvement. That's important—but it's not what we're talking about here. We're talking about a broader and more expansive dialogue that drives development.

We've just discussed the value of hindsight conversations, which surface essential information from the employee's point of view. The problem is that the individual's perspective is rarely a complete picture. The employee needs a reality check—an opportunity to expand their perspective beyond their own and to round out their self-assessment. Voilà! An opportunity for feedback.

Helping employees to proactively solicit the points of view of others offers them many benefits:

► They're able to check their assumptions, expand their understanding of themselves, and discover who they are in the eyes of others.

► They develop the capacity to independently initiate feedback conversations.

▶ They build stronger, more collaborative, and trust-based relationships with others.

Do this well enough for long enough and pretty soon you'll have a self-generating feeding frenzy—in a good way—in which employees become comfortable getting and volunteering feedback freely among themselves.

WHO'S WHO IN THEIR ZOO

Feedback is another sort of a hindsight conversation. The good, the bad, and the ugly need to be confirmed or dispelled as the employee's perspective is checked against the points of view held by others.

To ensure the most complete picture, it's important to tap into the broadest career audience possible. Ask employees who might have additional insight into them, their strengths, abilities, interests, and opportunities.

The answer will likely include some combination of

▶ Peers	▶ Interns	▶ Family
▶ Employees	▶ Customers	▶ Friends
▶ Contractors	▶ Suppliers	▶ Manager

You'll notice that you—the manager—are last on the list. And that's to make a point.

When it comes to **career development,** it takes a **village.**

Employees need to develop the broadest network possible to facilitate their career success. Co-workers and others within and outside the organization have potentially important information, ideas, and helpful contacts. And gathering feedback from them is an ideal way for employees to begin to take ownership for their careers and engage others in creating paths forward.

As the manager, you have a unique perspective. But yours is one of many that will inform the employee's understanding of themselves and help to be the basis for effective career development and planning.

Encourage employees to gather feedback from others before sharing your own. It's not about politeness (e.g., letting the guests get their food first) but about power. You've got it and, as a result, your perspective may carry undue weight. When employees come to you with a plate full of feedback from others, they are better able to put your perspective into perspective.

JUST REMEMBER: ABC

Soliciting and accepting feedback graciously are skills that distinguish successful and effective individuals. Yet many people have not had the benefit of learning these skills. Your employees are likely among them.

Since the act of opening one's self up to the opinions of others can be challenging, the agenda for such a discussion should be simple—as straightforward as ABC. Encourage employees to focus on just three things as they gather feedback from others: abilities, blind spots, and conditions.

Abilities

► What are my greatest strengths?

► Which of my skills are most valuable?

► What can you always count on me for?

► What value do I bring?

Blind Spots

▶ What behaviors have you observed that might get in my way?

▶ How have I fallen short of expectations?

▶ How might my strengths work against me?

▶ What one change could I make that would have the greatest positive effect on my success?

Conditions

▶ In what settings or under what circumstances do I make the greatest contributions?

▶ Under what conditions have you observed me struggling?

▶ Do I tend to perform best when working with others or flying solo?

▶ What factors have you noticed trigger stress or other negative reactions for me?

These specific, concrete questions demand more specific, concrete responses. They generate considerably more actionable information than the lazy feedback default question "How am I doing?"—which normally generates a tepid thumbs up.

So work with employees to select a question or two from each category to use as the starting point for feedback conversations with individuals in their career networks.

Then, be prepared to debrief these conversations. At first, people might need help overcoming the natural human response to focus on the data that validates their existing world view. They may need help evaluating multiple perspectives to recognize and identify common threads and themes. They may need help making sense of seemingly contradictory information. Investing time with others to process feedback sends a strong message to employees and provides you with additional information to support that person's growth.

As you can imagine, live, face-to-face feedback conversations are ideal. But, given today's distributed workforce, employees may need to

Raw, real human

conversation

can be the most direct **path** to greater **awareness** and stronger **relationships**, even when it's unrehearsed and clumsy— perhaps **especially** when it's unrehearsed and clumsy!

resort to virtual means—phone or web chat. Whatever form it takes, this sort of real-time interaction can surface valuable information while strengthening relationships.

Greater awareness and stronger relationships support career development. In this way, feedback really does help employees grow where they are, so they won't go and grow somewhere else. As a bonus, they develop a critical skill that leads to greater success on the job and in life.

And, if you have an online tool that you love, keep using it—in addition to, not *instead of*, conversation.

CHECK YOUR INTENTIONS

You might have been at the end of that list of those who provide feedback, but you're not forgotten. You are a critical part of your employees' career audience too, which means that they'll be looking to you to share your perspective as well as your opinions about their abilities, blind spots, and the conditions that support their success. Your role is to be your employees' honest advocate, someone they can count on for candor but also for support.

❝I can hear almost anything she has to say because I know deep down that she's on my side.❞

—Registered nurse

But before you earn the right to offer feedback that others will take to heart, it's essential to do an intention check. The verbal formula you follow when delivering feedback matters less than the intentions you bring to the conversation. The motivation of the feedback-giver totally trumps technique. The spirit of the message overrides its syntax. What comes from the heart overshadows what comes out of our mouths.

When getting ready to offer feedback, ask yourself, *What's my intention?* If it's to get something off your chest or make someone else wrong, you might want to think twice. Your intentions speak considerably louder than the words you choose. So make sure that all feedback is rooted in a sincere desire to be of service to someone's growth.

Intention + Information = Inspiration

When you marry a positive intent with well-chosen words, you create an unbeatable platform for helping others absorb, understand, and take action based on your feedback.

FRAME YOUR FEEDBACK

Organizing your thoughts and words for optimal impact can be as easy as following these three steps.

1. **Focus on the *what*.** The *what* refers to the specific, concrete behaviors and results that have a bearing on the employee's career direction and progression. Be as specific as you can be, sharing the details necessary to ensure a complete understanding. But, don't stop there.

2. **Follow up with *so what*.** Explore the impact of the behavior and results you highlight. This provides a context for your feedback and helps the employee make sense of your feedback in terms of career development and direction.

   ► **Don't say:** You're a great rep. Keep up the good work.

   ► **Do say:** You consistently offer creative solutions to our customers' problems. Your behavior is the standard that new reps see and emulate. You're becoming a real leader of the team.

3. **Explore the *now what*.** Feedback—whether positive or negative—offers an opportunity for reflection and possible action. If the feedback validates what the employee is currently doing, it's a chance to consider how to build upon success or leverage strengths in new ways. If the feedback suggests opportunities for improvement, it's a chance to make different choices or learn new skills and approaches. In either case, the key is for you to ask insightful questions like:

► What's your reaction to this?

► What does this mean to you?

► What do you want to do with this information?

► What steps might you consider taking?

► What's in it for you to take these steps or make these changes?

► Whose help might you recruit?

► What support do you need?

This simple framework—when combined with your positive intention—offers a multipurpose roadmap that supports career conversations, performance feedback, and even clear, actionable communication outside of the workplace.

USE CANDOR AND CARE

This is not an either/or choice. It's both/and. Employees care deeply about what their managers feel and think about them. As a result, their ability to hear a tough message is directly proportionate to the care with which you deliver it. The few minutes you take to consider and frame your feedback can make a tremendous difference in terms of its reception and usefulness.

► **Don't say:** You just don't seem to be able to cut it in sales.

► **Do say:** You have the ability to develop strong relationships with customers. Those relationships, though, aren't translating into sales. Let's talk about where your strengths can be better used.

Brain researchers found that people experience the same physiological responses to feedback that they do to physical threats. (You probably could have told them that based on how the mere mention of "feedback" makes your heart pound a bit faster and the moisture in your mouth suddenly finds its way to your brow.) Leading with strengths, talents, and skills can create greater psychological safety and help others remain more present and receptive to the more sensitive information you have to share.

" Most people want to hear the truth, even if it is unpalatable—
there is something within us that responds deeply to people
who level with us. **"**

—Susan Scott, author of *Fierce Conversations*

WHAT ABOUT YOU? ·

How frequently do you seek out feedback from others? How receptive are you to information about your performance or behavior?
How gracious and appreciative are you when someone points out
something you could do better? You set the tone for your team. A
feedback-rich culture begins with you. Do you want a free flow of
feedback? Start modeling what it looks like to solicit, welcome, and
use feedback from others.

A FEEDBACK FOCUS

Don't know where to start? Or do you want to expand your feedback
focus to better support your employees' growth? Look no further.
Employees need to get information from you around three key areas:
technical skills, soft skills, and a set of career intangibles.

Technical or hard skills are those that relate specifically to how
employees produce the outputs of their jobs. Whether it's welding or
website design, selling or shift management, hard skills are the funda-
mentals of performing one's work—and what we typically think of first
when we consider what's needed to be successful in a role and beyond.

But, that's just the tip of the iceberg. What's equally important (more
important according to some) is the set of interpersonal or soft skills
that enable someone's success. This includes communication, collaboration, teamwork, and networking. And anyone who's ever struggled to
master them knows that these soft skills can be pretty hard.

There's yet another category of intangibles that are frequently forgotten. They operate below the surface as a set of often-unconscious competencies. Forty years of field research has found that these qualities are key differentiators when it comes to day-to-day and long-term career success:

▶ Thirst for continuous learning

▶ Constant curiosity about the world and the possibilities it holds

▶ Sincere interest in continuing the journey toward self-awareness

▶ Resilience in the face of challenges and change

While people may be hardwired with a greater or lesser tendency toward these intangibles, these skills can definitely be developed over time—and with your supportive feedback.

Address any of these areas—technical skills, soft skills, or career intangibles—and you'll deepen self-awareness and plant important developmental seeds. Combine a couple for a powerful and enlightening conversation. Add them all to your list of possible feedback topics to address over time as you share your perspective in support of your employees' growth.

What IF . . .

▶ everyone enjoyed clarity about who they are, what they're good at, where opportunities to improve exist, and where they could make the greatest difference?

▶ employees felt comfortable receiving feedback?

▶ managers were not the only ones empowered and able to provide feedback?

5

What's Happening

Telling me that the business landscape is changing is like telling an Eskimo it's cold outside. I know. I live it. But there's got to be a better way than always scrambling and reacting. I don't want to just keep up—I want to get ahead of the curve.

—An employee (perhaps yours)

We are not going to tell you the world is changing. You could write that book. The changes and challenges you face every day frame your decisions about strategy, resource allocation, and other critical business matters.

Shouldn't they frame career decisions as well? (Answer: a resounding yes.)

Hindsight conversations provide a solid grounding in who the full person really is and what they bring to the party. But pursuing career growth with this clarity alone is a very dangerous proposition. It can send people in directions that are interesting and may play to their strengths—but it might not necessarily serve a business need. (Read: dead ends.)

Hindsight clarity must be filtered through the lens of foresight. Foresight conversations open people's minds to the broader world, the future, organizational issues, changes, and the implications of all of these. Foresight helps others focus their career efforts in ways that will lead to satisfying and productive outcomes. (It also delivers the benefit of context and perspective that enhances day-to-day work.)

BEYOND THE CRYSTAL BALL

We've all heard stories about individuals who allowed their skills to become rusty and themselves to become irrelevant. But what about those who anticipated the future and were ready to grow into it? These

Some people have an innate **ability** to keep their **eyes open** to the world around them.

To **spot trends** where others see u•n•c•o•n•n•e•c•t•e•d d•o•t•s.

To play out the implications of a **seemingly** insignificant event.

are the high-profile examples of business legends. But there are also the mere mortals who work on the ground floor and seem to have the gift of living just a little further out in the future than the rest of us.

These people are probably not psychics. But they do practice their own brand of ESP: Ever Scanning and Pondering.

While it may come naturally to some, you can nurture it in others. ESP is a set of habits—habits that you can help employees build through ongoing foresight conversations.

FOSTERING FORESIGHT

You've been to the meetings (or not) and read the memos (or not). You know the big picture for your organization (or not). You may lay awake at night worrying about it or you've so internalized it that it's always operating under the surface, unconsciously informing much of what you do. But many employees have little visibility to this information and may not appreciate its importance.

So populate their radar screens with a constellation of new points to consider:

▶ External challenges and changes—what's going on in the world— including changing demographics, globalization, competition, government regulation, geopolitical forces, and economic shifts

▶ Internal challenges and changes—what's going on within the orga- nization—including changing customer expectations, new vendor relationships, mergers and acquisitions, the evolving employment landscape, and responses to shrinking margins

"Don't seat me at the kids' table. I might not be an executive, but I know there are changes coming. Let me in on things. I deserve to know, whether I can do anything about it or not."

—Production worker

Don't worry—we're not suggesting that you deliver a whole strategic planning curriculum to your staff. On the contrary, we're just suggesting that you create a forum for employees to get in touch with the world around them—the world that defines their career development playing fields.

▶ TRY THIS: HARNESS MORE HEADS
. . . .

Whereas most career conversations are personal, one-on-one interactions between the employee and manager, foresight conversations are best enjoyed by a group. (And you'll enjoy the efficiency of this approach.)

Get your team gathering information, researching issues, and having direct experiences that deliver a visceral understanding of business changes and challenges. In this case, two, three, four, or more heads are better than one.

Nobody can be an expert on all of the forces and factors shaping the world, business, or your organization—not even you. So let the wisdom of your crowd take over. Encourage the activities and conversations that will help all employees develop the ESP habit.

Here's a starter list of ways people can begin to develop a visceral understanding of what's happening in the world around them. But between you and your employees, you'll likely come up with plenty more.

▶ Interview key individuals

▶ Engage in focused customer contact

▶ Research important issues or trends

▶ Read trade publications

▶ Participate in industry conferences

▶ Attend management or other cross-functional meetings

These activities will spark awareness and insight about the bigger picture—that is, what's going on in the world, the industry, and the organization itself. But the conversation and following reflection

Individual puzzle pieces don't look like much. Put them together and you've got the complete picture.

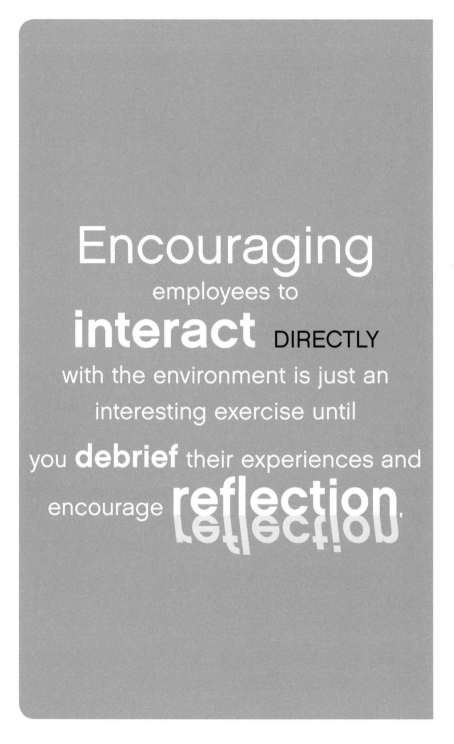

Encouraging employees to **interact** DIRECTLY with the environment is just an interesting exercise until you **debrief** their experiences and encourage **reflection**.

translates insight into a deep and useful understanding of the issues and their implications.

Simple questions that help people connect the dots go a long way:

▶ What are some of the most important things you learned?

▶ What might these things mean to our industry?

▶ What might they mean to our organization?

▶ How might they affect our products/services/revenue stream?

▶ How might they impact our department?

▶ What do they mean for you, your job, your career goals?

FORESIGHT FORUMS

Really want to make a difference? Consider institutionalizing foresight conversations by putting them on every meeting agenda. If you did this even occasionally, it would help, and you'd be doing more than most managers. Have employees report on what they've learned. Hold an open discussion using the questions listed earlier.

❝❝I started asking different staff members to kick off our meetings with a brief headline review—something from a trade publication, business journal, or general news. They gave a two-minute overview of the article and led a brief discussion about what it meant to us. I was surprised by the insights the group generated and how engaged they became. One week I forgot to include it on the agenda—and they let me know about it.❞❞

—Risk manager

Imagine what could happen if you started each staff meeting with a focus on foresight. The results would be powerful. Every employee would develop greater clarity that would help to inform career development and decisions.

But you'll soon discover that this is only part of the benefits of group foresight conversations. You'll learn more than you might expect.

Employees will begin acting like business partners. You may even see more innovation and better results. Who knows what you'll accomplish...world peace? (That last one was just to make sure you were paying attention.)

► TRY THIS: FILL IN THE BLANKS

Another approach to engaging employees in big-picture conversations is just to set aside a few minutes and ask them to complete provocative sentence stems, such as

- ► The most significant change I've seen in our industry is...
- ► I predict that the next big thing will be...
- ► I can imagine a time when...
- ► Our business would be turned upside down if...
- ► Everything will change with the obsolescence of...
- ► I was most personally affected when the organization changed...
- ► It really made a difference when management...
- ► To keep my edge and pursue my career goals, I'm going to need to...

Pick one or more. Do it individually. Or do it with the team as a whole. And watch the conversation unfold.

Don't be fooled. These sentence stems are as powerful as they are simple. They force employees—sometimes for the first time—to step back and think more broadly and strategically about the world around them and what it means for their careers.

WHAT ABOUT YOU?

Consider these sentence stems yourself. How would you complete them? What do your responses mean in terms of what you'd like to be doing with your career?

DISRUPT OR BE DISRUPTED

We don't need to tell you that products and services that are viable today can become obsolete tomorrow. In response to this challenging and unpredictable reality, most organizations include innovation as a key strategic objective. But mere incrementalism may not be sufficient to survive and thrive. Disruption or radical change is the new normal. Organizations can certainly choose not to proactively disrupt; but, in that case, they'd better prepare to be disrupted themselves.

Even the employment landscape reflects this disruptive dynamic. The workplace of the past was completely populated with full-time employees. Today, it's a patchwork quilt of badge types and employment forms—full-time, part-time, contractor, consultant, intern, extern...and the list goes on.

Individual responses to all of this disruption depend in large part upon our point of view. Is the glass half scary or half exciting? Disruption brings with it new challenges, accelerated learning, and sustainable engagement. Particularly as employees live and work longer, disruption offers the opportunity to retain your people by keeping them interested and growing right where they are.

Embracing disruption and the massive opportunities that come with it requires employees to be ready, receptive, and resilient. Whether someone comes out feeling vulnerable or victorious depends largely upon one thing: their level of agility.

THE AGILE ADVANTAGE

At its core, agility is all about staying current, keeping pace, shifting gears, responding fluidly—and doing it all nimbly and quickly. It's about preparing one's self to remain in a perpetual state of readiness to perceive and pivot toward possibilities. Agility is the secret sauce of sustainable success.

While *foresight* offers an understanding of what's happening within the bigger picture and why, *agility* offers the ability to leverage that understanding—to make it work in your favor by taking smart and responsive actions. And, you'll notice we use the word *actions* here—in its plural form. Given the dynamic and disruptive nature of today's workplace, singular paths forward must give way to multiple concurrent strategies and steps. This mitigates risk and offers the flexibility required to navigate quickly shifting conditions. Because when it comes to business and careers, everyone needs to keep their options open.

So hindsight is powerful but incomplete without the overlay of foresight. What's happening in the changing world around us plays directly into career decisions, strategies, and success. Agile employees can make the disruptions and changes work for them with the help of some new habits—habits built and instilled through foresight conversations.

The intersection between hindsight and foresight is insight.

HINDSIGHT   FORESIGHT

INSIGHT

And the possible insights are endless:

► A new skill might be deployed to solve a problem.

► Evolving interests might support a new business direction.

► A long-held goal might be pursued through a vital project.

Insights that are recognized, explored, and exploited through career conversations with employees could uncover countless possibilities that will help them grow.

What IF . . .

► employees could develop the habit of scanning and pondering the environment around them?

► foresight conversations were a part of day-to-day life in your organization?

► disruption was welcomed as an opportunity for individual and organizational growth?

6

If Not

Then What?

Challenge me. Stretch me. I'm not as worried about being promoted as I am about learning, growing, and seeing my talents used in new and different ways.

—An employee (perhaps yours)

Insight and growth are all about possibilities. But the problem is that managers and employees alike frequently have an outdated view of what those possibilities are. Growth in today's business environment means bidding adieu to some old thinking.

Say good-bye to the career ladder. Organizational belt-tightening and delayering continue to eat away at the leadership headcount in most organizations. The upper layers of the pyramid (which have always been slimmer) have become a mere sliver.

Say good-bye to limiting career paths. The predictable progression from one established position to the next has given way to career patterns. These are more fluid, flexible, and responsive to the needs of the business and the individual.

Say good-bye to checking your personal life at the door. We've moved beyond work/life balance to work/life integration. The convergence of technology and communication has blurred the lines for many between work and home.

A growing number of workers have come to the realization that they can't have it all—or at least not all at one time—and are not willing to sacrifice important parts of their lives for a job. Increasingly, people are deciding that work has to work for them.

Say hello to a new way of thinking about how careers happen—through possible moves around, down, up, over…or the decision to strategically develop in place.

Today's career development looks more like a rock-climbing wall than a ladder.

Climbing Wall Wisdom 1—The top doesn't have to be the goal. Frequently, getting across or to a specific spot is exactly what you're looking to achieve.

"I'm happy at my current level. I don't ever want the headaches of being the boss. But I also don't want to stagnate where I am. I need to keep figuring out the next challenge, the next place I can make things happen."

—Technician

Climbing Wall Wisdom 2—There are countless ways to get from point A to point B.

"I've reinvented myself several times over my career. Moving from sales to operations and now to customer service sure wasn't the straightest path, but I picked up exactly what I needed along the way."

—Customer service supervisor

Climbing Wall Wisdom 3—Sometimes getting to your ultimate destination requires a move down the wall a bit.

"I really wanted to work in product development but knew I'd never be successful (or even considered) because I hadn't spent time in the trenches with the customer. So I consciously downgraded my job title to get the experience that I needed. And, it all paid off in the end."

—Product manager

Climbing Wall Wisdom 4—You can choose safer or riskier moves, more or less secure footholds and handholds, depending upon the conditions that present themselves.

“ When my youngest child became ill, I knew I couldn't keep up with the demands of my business development group. I had to make a decision. I'm grateful that my manager was open to helping me find another position with more regular hours. Now that everything is settled at home again, I'm happy to be back to my previous frenetic pace. ”

—Director, business development

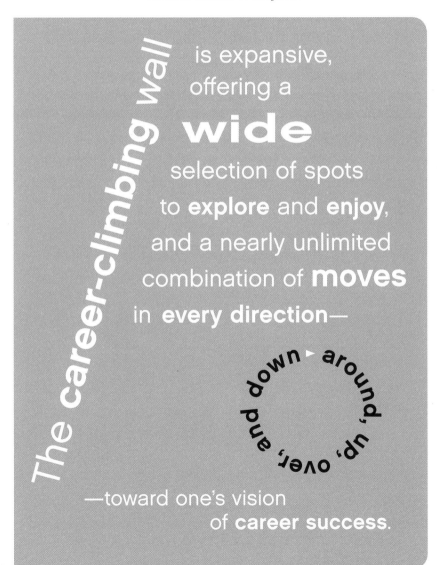

The career-climbing wall is expansive, offering a **wide** selection of spots to **explore** and **enjoy**, and a nearly unlimited combination of **moves** in **every direction**—

down ► around, up, over, and

—toward one's vision of **career success**.

Climbing Wall Wisdom 5 — Depending upon your choice of handholds and footholds, you can cultivate strength, skill, and interest without making a move.

" In my business, there's an overwhelming number of tools, instruments, and different client needs. When I master where I am now and feel ready for the next challenge, I won't need to change roles. I'll just turn my attention to getting up to speed on the new product line and bringing that into my practice. "

—IT lead

Onward and *upward* has been replaced by **forward** ▶ and ▶ **toward**.

ADVANCING THE NOTION OF ADVANCEMENT

The climbing wall metaphor only works if we shift our mindset about what career progression and advancement really mean in today's environment.

We've been brainwashed into thinking that *advancement* means moving up in the organization: taking on more responsibility, managing larger staffs, and earning more money.

Advancement today means moving forward and toward one's very personal definition of career success—which in many cases requires no movement at all.

Do you know

► How your employees define career success?

► What kind of work they want to be doing?

► What they want to achieve?

► What talents they yearn to leverage or activate?

WHAT ABOUT YOU?

Ask yourself the same questions:

► How do you define career success for yourself?

► What kind of work do you want to be doing?

► What do you want to achieve?

► What talents do you yearn to leverage or activate?

You're in good company if you struggled with your own answers. You're in even better company if you don't know how your employees would answer. So is it any wonder that career development is challenging? Most managers are flying blind.

Employees need to come to terms with how they personally define *career success* and recast that as *advancement*. And they need to let you in on that secret if they want your help and support.

As a result, some of the most important conversations you'll have with employees involve clarifying their definition of career success. A profound and thoughtful dialogue can be sparked by asking simple questions, such as

► What do you want to be doing?

► How do you want to be doing it?

► With whom and under what circumstances?

There simply is no cookie-cutter approach for the customized, personalized, tailored, just-for-me plan that advances each employee's unique career goals.

This is the part where you're thinking, "I knew that eventually it would get around to all the work I have to do to manage my employee's career." Right? Wrong.

Let's be clear: It's your job to facilitate the conversations that inspire insights, awareness, and action on the part of the employee. You take the lead in the talk—asking, guiding, reflecting, exploring. But they own the action.

UP, DOWN, AND ALL AROUND

Understanding the employee's definition of *career success* is the first step. Pursuing that definition can happen through any number of moves in a variety of different directions. Getting there may mean

► Promotions to higher positions

► Lateral adjustments

► Steps that gain valuable experience that in the past might have been considered down or backward

► Alternative working arrangements such as shifting to contractor, consultant, part-time, or other contingent employment status

► Even growing in place (adapted from *CareerPower*, Career Systems International, 2011)

Up is what immediately comes to most people's minds when they think about career advancement. And, although there may be fewer opportunities closer to the top, vertical moves remain important and necessary. Organizations thrive when they have a pipeline filled with skilled internal candidates prepared to take on the challenges of the next level.

But, up is not the only way to go for employees looking for growth. In fact, in these days of flatter organizations, a lateral move is often the new promotion.

Increasingly, becoming knowledgeable about more of the organization is an asset. Taking on a role at a similar level on the org chart broadens perspective. It encourages a more holistic view of the business. It activates a new and expanded network. And it builds agility, which is king in today's economy.

Recalibration is another option, although it won't win popularity contests with employees. How can you help others understand that moving from one level to another that may be considered lower organizationally is valid, honorable, and frequently strategic? (Answer: begin by delivering it yourself.)

Managers have to help employees see that it's **not**

down shifting.

It's just changing lanes, sometimes avoiding the traffic, and seeing new scenery in the process.

Sometimes the smartest move—and the fastest way forward—is to intentionally step back.

> **"**I saw the writing on the wall. My division had a first-class ticket to outsourcing. I wanted to stay with the company—and looked forward to leading bigger projects eventually. So I moved over to another division. I went from managing three people to being an individual contributor again. I have to be honest—my ego took a hit for a while. But, I established myself quickly and learned a lot about a whole new group of customers. It was exactly what I needed to get me where I am today.**"**
>
> —Engineer

It can be a hard sell—but recalibration is frequently the best way for employees to progress forward toward their goals.

There's also the option of growing in place. But this option is so rich and filled with opportunities that it gets its own chapter...so read on.

Clearly, *up* is not the only way. And even if up is the preferred destination, the climbing wall—the business environment in which we all operate—offers lots of ways to get there.

What IF . . .

▶ you had a clear understanding of how each employee uniquely defines career success?

▶ employees viewed career advancement and development more like a rock-climbing wall than a ladder?

▶ everyone pursued their career goals through a nearly unlimited combination of moves—over, around, up, and down?

▶ developing in place became the popular and sought-after strategy for growth?

7

Same Seat, New View

My friend worked for the same boss in the same department for nearly seven years. Sounds mind numbing, right? For him, it was anything but. His manager encouraged him to keep changing it up, helped him develop and really use his talents in all sorts of new ways. He grew way more than I did, even changing jobs every couple of years. That's the kind of manager I want.

—An employee (perhaps yours)

Be honest. All that talk of insight, possibilities, recalibration, and upward and lateral moves in the last chapter made you a little nervous didn't it? As much as you'd like to help your employees transition into new roles that will support their growth goals, it's not always possible.

And that's why too many managers avoid career discussions altogether. You don't want to set unrealistic expectations only to disappoint when desirable moves are few and far between.

THINK GLOBAL, ACT LOCAL

Hindsight and foresight overlap to reveal insights into a whole world of development possibilities that exist for employees. Some involve moves, but (and here's the best-kept secret that will liberate development-minded managers everywhere) the vast majority do not.

Growth is not now and has never been limited to movements over, up, or down. But somehow that expectation has gotten a lot more air-time than it deserves. With the right support, people can grow right where they're planted.

Growth in place is the most accessible yet most underutilized career development strategy available to managers. Let's face it. You may have little influence over getting an employee transferred or promoted, but you are completely in charge of what goes on in your own backyard. Finding ways to grow talents, explore interests, and build capacity within the context of one's current job is completely within your sphere of influence.

Do you want to

► Raise engagement levels?

► Uncover and activate previously unknown or underutilized talents that can help the business?

► Retain top talent by keeping work interesting?

► Establish a culture of continuous learning and development?

► Build the skills and knowledge needed so employees will be prepared when broader moves become available?

► Generate loyalty and the kind of leadership reputation that will have the best talent standing in line to work for you?

Help employees move forward and toward their career goals without making a move. Help them grow in place. Making this happen requires a shift in mindset.

TANGLED IN TITLES

Remember as a kid how adults were always asking what you wanted to be when you grew up? Astronaut. Designer. Doctor. We've been programmed since childhood to think in terms of *being*. And this is reinforced in the workplace as the org chart defines what we want to be—sending us to chase after a progression of positions and titles.

But we know that given today's reality, there just may not be that many positions or titles available. Does it mean that people who remain in the same role are condemned to pickling their minds, extinguishing their spirits, and not developing? (Answer: absolutely not.)

What it means is that managers must shift the conversation from what employees want to *be* to what they want to *do*.

► What kind of work do you want to be doing?

► What problems do you want to solve?

► What challenges do you want to confront?

► What kinds of materials, issues, customers do you want to deal with?

► What achievements do you want to attain?

► What legacy do you want to leave?

"I figured out a long time ago that the job title doesn't mean nearly as much as the richness of the experiences it offers. Titles belong on books—not on people."

—Retail supervisor

Discussions around what people want to be are inherently limiting. There will likely never be enough promotions and moves to go around. But discussions about what people want to do are constrained only by the creativity that you and the employee bring to them. A savvy manager can always find ways to invite greater challenge and interest into the envelope of someone's current role.

The **challenge** of
growing in place
involves stripping titles
from our thinking and instead
focusing on what the employee
needs to experience, know,
learn, and be able to do.

> When you **reframe** development in terms of identifying and sourcing necessary **experiences**, you **widen** the lens of **possibilities** and allow your people to grow right where they are.

Focusing more on *doing* and less on *being* offers employees a way to expand their definitions of career success in a way that allows for greater development in place. This mindset and approach acknowledges the reality of the current workplace while meeting the needs of the employee and the organization at the same time.

"It was a head scratcher at first. My technical documentation specialist announced that she wanted to become a nonprofit grant writer. We didn't have a lot of need for that in our for-profit manufacturing plant. But after thinking about it together, we realized that there were several skill areas shared by both roles. We figured out a way for her to develop her writing skills to improve the quality of her current projects and prepare her for creating grants. And she spent some time in sales helping to write proposals and other influence pieces. As a result, her engagement and commitment grew—and now she does some volunteer grant writing on the side.**"**

—Documentation manager

Managers who successfully support others growing in place are opportunity minded. Are you?

WHAT ABOUT YOU? •

Do you

See people as interesting, complex, and multidimensional?	❑ YES	❑ NO
Pick up on cues that employees are ready for something more?	❑ YES	❑ NO
Spot strengths that can be used in different or unusual ways?	❑ YES	❑ NO
See multiple ways of getting work done?	❑ YES	❑ NO
Squeeze learning from nearly every experience and interaction?	❑ YES	❑ NO
Cringe when you hear someone say, "But that's not how we do it around here"?	❑ YES	❑ NO
View job descriptions as helpful guidelines rather than handcuffs?	❑ YES	❑ NO
Take pleasure in finding ways to maximize talent?	❑ YES	❑ NO
Feel energized by thinking outside of the box?	❑ YES	❑ NO
Resist seeing the world in terms of round pegs and square holes?	❑ YES	❑ NO

Analysis

► If you answered *yes* eight or more times, you are an opportunity visionary with 20/20 vision when it comes to finding ways to help employees seek out the circumstances they need to gain important skills, knowledge, and experiences.

► If you answered *yes* five to seven times, you are opportunity minded and frequently see ways to connect your employees' career advancement needs with opportunities within the organization.

▶ If you answered *yes* four or fewer times, you may find that you are turning a blind eye toward opportunities to help your employees advance.

See *Love 'Em or Lose 'Em: Getting Good People to Stay* (Berrett-Koehler, 2014) for more on opportunity mindedness.

Opportunity is defined as a set of circumstances that makes it possible to do something—in this case, it involves helping others move forward and toward their definition of career success while finding ways to do what interests them most.

Opportunity-minded managers **envision** and **enable** possibility-advancing **circumstances** with **employees**—through **conversation**.

But even opportunity-minded managers fall prey to an all-too-common mistake. They jump directly from employees' definitions of success or descriptions of what they want to do to "Here's what we're gonna do." It's natural. As a manager, you didn't get to where you are by not being action oriented.

Moving prematurely to action causes you to shoehorn the possible into the practical far too early. It also

► Sidesteps important thinking

► Chokes off creativity

► Jumps to solutions before you know what the opportunity is

► Narrows the conversation

► Blinds you to the full range of possibilities

So instead, slow down a bit. Explore what the employees need to know or be capable of, so they can *do* what interests them most. Consider the skills, information, and abilities that will enable success. Crystalize these needs and priorities before jumping to action.

► TRY THIS: FIRST THINGS FIRST

Agree with the employee that you'll both suspend all talk of *how* to achieve what's needed. Instead, focus jointly on determining *what* is required for helping your employee move forward. Questions like these open up the possibilities:

► To reach your goal, what skills and knowledge will you need?

► How can you get ready for what you want to do?

► What capabilities will prepare you to be successful?

► What gaps might currently exist?

► What do you need to learn?

► What skills might you want to acquire?

► What might you need more of?

► What might you need less of?

GUIDE TOWARD

GUIDE AWAY FROM

What you're looking for during this conversation are these kinds of responses:

▶ I need to broaden my business exposure.

▶ I've got to get more experience in different situations.

▶ I'd really benefit from getting closer to the customer.

▶ Developing a global perspective—that's what I need.

▶ I need to get some P&L responsibility under my belt.

▶ Can you help me create a strong support network?

▶ I'll have to increase the complexity of the leadership challenges I face.

What you're *not* looking for are these kinds of responses:

▶ I have to manage the customer care department.

▶ You've got to transfer me to John's group.

▶ Please enroll me in the next management training series.

▶ I'd like your job, thanks for asking.

These sorts of responses are signals that the employee is jumping to solutions before fully exploring the problem, opportunity, or gap.

Together, generate a broad pool of skills, abilities, and information that will support employees to move forward and toward their definitions of success. Opportunity-minded managers know how to make this happen.

IN A WORD

The opportunity minded share a whole language that shines a light on the nearly unlimited ways people can grow in place. Don't know the language? Use this development dictionary.

These are powerful words. They are synonymous with growth. They get people thinking. They point employees in new and sometimes invisible directions. They establish or maintain momentum forward and toward the employee's career goals. This list is just the beginning!

THE DEVELOPMENT DICTIONARY

Reconsider Experiment
Raise
Learn Sharpen Specialize
Deepen
Expand Spread Extend Reinforce
Communicate Observe
Research
Challenge Broaden
Minimize Add Decrease
Seek Strengthen Return
Share Multiply Revive
Observe Intensify
Cultivate Test Look
Increase Practice Reenergize
Enhance Refresh

► TRY THIS: OPPORTUNITY WORD SEARCH
. . . .

1. Share the Development Dictionary with employees to spark thinking about the skills, capabilities, and information required to move forward and toward their definitions of career success, which involves doing what interests them most.

2. Ask employees to pick as many words as apply and to use them as starters for phrases that describe what they need or want. (Example: "I need to broaden my network of resources," or "I want to sharpen my negotiating skills.")

3. Based upon your understanding of the opportunity, have a few ideas in your hip pocket to offer as well.

4. Discuss each to clarify and identify additional needs.

Approaching the conversation in this way reframes opportunities for development, moving away from titles and promotions and toward a more doable focus. It offers fodder for growth in the here-and-now, leveraging the current role rather than waiting for some future promotion that might or might not ever come. And it enriches the experience, engagement, and growth of those employees who—perhaps not interested in a promotion—might have passed on the opportunity for development.

WHAT ABOUT YOU? . . . .
Which words appeal to you? What ideas do they prompt around what you need or want to develop your own career?
. . . .

This is how you become fluent in the language of *developing in place*—and how you can recognize countless ways to help people see a brand-new view without ever having to move.

What IF . . .

▶ employees didn't think of their careers in terms of a litany of roles and titles?

▶ managers made the most of what they control: opportunities to grow within the division, department, or role?

▶ everyone became even just a little more opportunity minded?

▶ developing in place became as attractive, interesting, and respected as other options?

. . . .

8

Advancing Action

We go through the exercise every year. Spend a bunch of time figuring out *what* I need to develop my career. Time's typically up just about when we get around to *how* to make it happen. I honestly think this does more harm than good. It's like a tease that gives me a hint of what's possible then slams the door on it—until next year, when we do it all over again.

—An employee (perhaps yours)

The work you do with employees around hindsight and foresight helps to generate insight into the world of possibilities that exist for those who want to move forward and toward their career goals. Identifying those possibilities is exciting and energizing—whether they involve preparing for a move or developing in place. But those possibilities remain high level and abstract until they translate to action.

This translation doesn't happen magically or by chance. Rather, it happens through intentional effort—and intentional conversation between you and your employees.

Whether your employees wish to refresh their knowledge of a technical system, practice new work processes, sharpen their ability to identify the best deals, extend their knowledge of one product line to another, strengthen interpersonal skills, or any other developmental priority, you have three primary ways to make it happen.

▶ TRY THIS

To learn more about the developmental strategies available to you (and your own go-to preferences), review the learning activities on the next page. Circle the three or four approaches you have used most frequently and effectively to learn and to grow.

Circle the three or four approaches you have used most frequently and effectively to learn and to grow.

Special projects

Information interviews

Action learning
(through projects/teams)

E-learning or webinars

Mentoring

👀 **OBSERVING others**

Job rotation Job rotation Job rotation Job rotation

Live workshops

Books and articles

Stretch assignments

JOB SHADOWING

Networking

Videos

Podcasts

Community service

The developmental activities you've gravitated toward in the past fall within one of three broad categories that are available for you to use with your employees. Make note of the colors of the learning activities you circled on the previous page. Were you drawn toward a majority of **black**, gray, or green items? And what might that mean?

▶ Education — the nearly unlimited sources of information and learning that can be formally or informally accessed.

▶ Exposure — the opportunities to learn from and through others via observation, mentorship, and more.

▶ Experience — action-based opportunities to learn by doing.

Understanding and using all of these strategies will allow you to work with employees to actually move from development insights and ideas to implementation.

From Cisco's adaptation of *The Career Architect Development Planner* by Michael M. Lomardo and Robert W. Eichenger (3rd edition, Minneapolis, MN: Lominger Ltd., 2000).

BACK TO SCHOOL

When people think of learning and development, they naturally think of education. For the majority of us, school is where we got most of our instruction and did most of our growing up.

In the workplace, education takes many forms—both old school and new school in nature. There are workshops on nearly any topic you can imagine. Community colleges offer credit and noncredit courses to build necessary knowledge and skills.

Education isn't limited to live-group settings though. For instance, e-learning and MOOCs (massive open online courses) allow for independent development whenever and wherever employees need it. TED Talks and other informative videos are available 24/7 for just-in-time, just-for-me learning. Online resources and tools abound. MIT provides its entire catalog of online courses free of charge. Webinars and virtual classrooms provide instruction while connecting people across the country or around the world.

► TRY THIS: ENABLE EDUCATION

It's easy to assume that if you've pointed employees in the right direction—or even signed them up for a class—that your role is over. After all,
it's up to them. Right? Wrong. People get the most value from education
when their managers help set them up for success. You'll see the best
results if you follow these steps.

1. Set expectations in advance. Through conversation, you can support
   employees to powerfully focus their effort and learning. Intentional
   learning is stimulated by good questions.

   ► How will this learning help move you forward and toward your
     career goals?

   ► What specifically do you hope to gain?

   ► How will you use what you've learned?

   ► What challenges or obstacles might come up as you learn?

   ► How will you address these challenges or obstacles?

   ► What are you willing to invest to make the most of this learn-
     ing opportunity?

   ► What do you need from me? (This one's optional, but only
     because many managers are afraid this will lead to a lengthy
     list of to-dos. Just try it. You'll be amazed at the small requests
     that can lead to disproportionately large returns on learning.)

2. Set aside time. Scheduling employees into classes is easy. Preserving
   that time so they can focus on the learning at hand—that's tougher.
   Nothing says "Your education and development don't matter" any
   louder than pulling people out of seminars, interrupting webinars,
   or letting other priorities preempt learning commitments. In fact, one
   of the biggest employee complaints is the discrepancy between what
   managers say about their commitment to learning and their behavior.
   So treat education like the real work that it is.

3. Set up opportunities to use what's learned. New skills and knowledge must be exercised to grow strong. Work with employees before, during, and after their educational experiences to find meaty and meaningful ways to apply, extend, and strengthen their learning.

4. Set a date to debrief. (More on this later.)

> **"Training used to be the panacea for everything. But with budget cuts and production pressures, managers are being more thoughtful about how to get the biggest bang from their employees' investment of time and money in training. They're getting more involved on the front end and the back end. And I think it's really paying off."**
>
> —Training director

EXPOSE WISDOM IN THE WORKPLACE

By now, you've probably learned the refrain of this book by heart: you don't have to do it all. Facilitate exposure by facilitating connections. The more individuals who are drawn into an employee's career support circle, the better.

> **"Once I realized that even if I had all the time in the world, I couldn't be all things to all people, it took a lot of pressure off. There are so many other people in the organization who are much better suited to help my folks learn what they need to know."**
>
> —Sales manager

Enabling exposure through mentoring, job shadowing, coaching, and networking costs virtually nothing. It can efficiently deliver learning as well as many more organizational outcomes. The key is to help employees determine who are the best resources available. Start the dialogue with such questions as

▶ Who is known for…?

▶ Which groups or teams have experience with…?

▶ Whose work do you admire in the area of…?

▶ Who might know someone who can help you learn more about…?

▶ Who's demonstrated skills and abilities around…?

AN UPDATED VIEW OF EXPOSURE

When employees are looking to learn and grow, they frequently focus on what they can get. That makes sense, but sometimes the most profound learning comes from what they can give.

In the past, mentoring was often conceived as a one-way, one-on-one transaction in which a more knowledgeable individual passed along wisdom, guidance, and insights around a body of knowledge to someone in need of learning. But in today's dynamic business environment, many people are challenging that old conception because

▶ Nobody knows it all. As a result, employees should strive to develop the broadest network possible of connections from whom they can learn. The past structure of one mentor to one protégé is history. The new model looks more like a mosaic of connections.

▶ It's reciprocal. Given the diversity in the workplace, there is something to be learned from nearly everyone we encounter. Enlightened mentors can learn as much as they teach.

❝My investment in mentoring younger associates is completely selfish. I might have more case experience and a deeper understanding of the law, but that's it. They have entirely new methods for gathering and organizing data that I'm trying to master. They aren't mired in the way we've always done things around here—and are always teaching me something new. I get way more than I give in these relationships.❞

—Attorney/senior partner

Teaching is sometimes the best way to learn. Progressive educators have known this for decades. So employees should look not just for people they can learn from, but also for those who can learn from *them*. Lessons in human dynamics, leadership, and communication are just the beginning.

Exposure in the form of mentoring, job shadowing, and networking is all about creating compelling connections among individuals who can share knowledge, skills, and experience. This could be peers, superiors, subordinates, people in other departments, or people outside the organization altogether. And the Internet exponentially expands the potential. You can open the door—and even your contact lists—but the employee has to walk through and take it from there.

Today, the lines between **mentoring** and **networking** are blurring. Welcome to the world of **mentworking**.

ENGINEER EXPERIENCES

Education and exposure go a long way toward helping employees develop. But experience is frequently the best and most powerful teacher.

Ask any five employees about the most important lessons they've learned and how they learned them. We predict that more than half didn't happen through education, training, or even other people. The key lessons happened through the experiences people had. (In many cases, the school of hard knocks.)

> **WHAT ABOUT YOU?**
>
> List the five most significant lessons you've learned. Trace each lesson back to where and when you learned it. How many were a result of education or exposure? If you're like most people, the vast majority of your learning has come through experience.

Experience-based learning is the Holy Grail for which many managers have been searching. Most people learn by doing. And there's a lot that needs to be done at work. Strategically bring the two together (someone with a learning need and authentic work assignments), and you can simultaneously serve the needs of the organization and the individual: a match made in heaven.

Experience-based learning is about integrating learning into the workflow. Some call it *embedded*; we just call it a sensible way to efficiently and effectively develop the talents of others.

"On-the-job learning is my personal favorite…in part due to its efficiency. Employees get what they need, and at the same time, we accomplish real work that matters.**"**

—Finance supervisor

Experience sounds like a big word. But don't be put off by it. Sending employees abroad or starting a new division for someone to head up are certainly experiences. But that's not what we're talking about here.

Experiences can be **scaled** based upon your **sphere of influence**, the **needs** of the **organization**, and what **employees** are looking to **achieve**.

And you have plenty of options—in fact, unlimited options—when you consider combinations and permutations of

► Stretch assignments

► Special projects

► Events

► In-department rotations

► Action learning projects and teams

► Job shadowing

► Community service

The most powerful and valuable development experiences involve hands-on, in-the-moment learning. There's no substitute for being confronted by and having to address real business challenges. And, given the number of challenges we face in business, the opportunity to leverage them is limited only by the imagination. Here are some examples.

If the development priority is to...	The experience might include...
▶ enhance understanding of how customers use the product/service	▶ conducting customer interviews, generating a summary report, and presenting findings at a department meeting
▶ cultivate supervisory and coaching skills	▶ working with all new hires to set expectations, develop job skills, and provide feedback and coaching
▶ broaden exposure to the challenges of delivering services in another territory	▶ standing in for an employee in another area while he or she is on leave

THE ZEN OF EXPERIENTIAL LEARNING

Without getting too deep, there are three truths that a manager must confront before helping people learn through experiences.

▶ With intention and attention, nearly any experience can drive learning and development. The activity doesn't need to be big or flashy. In fact, it can be quite small and insignificant. But learning is possible if the employee is focused on making it happen and reflecting on the lessons.

▶ There's no such thing as failure in a learning experience—only failure to learn from it. The quality of the outcome has little to do with the quality of the learning. In fact, according to some experts, humans learn more (and more quickly) through hardships and failure. The key is to help employees wring every bit of insight and learning from the experiences they have.

► Learning is a choice. And it's not yours. Employees must decide to actively engage and learn. You can help them think through how to do it, but they must take responsibility for the hard work of learning.

90%

of all great career-advancing

ideas go

nowhere.

Don't let the career-advancing ideas that you help your employees generate suffer that fate. Push those ideas just a little bit further, enough to make your conversations pay off.

LET'S MAKE A DEAL

Whatever combination of education, exposure, and experience you and your employee arrive at, there needs to be a plan—a plan that's hatched together through conversation. And the best plans are really collaborative development deals you strike with the employee. Make sure your DEAL is documented, employee owned, aligned with their goals, and linked to the needs of your organization.

Documented — Putting it in writing signals that this is significant and that you both are taking it seriously. It acts as a reminder to you and the employee and helps to drive follow-up. Write it on paper or electronically—rather than in concrete. That way you can treat the plan as the living, breathing, and changeable tool that it is.

Employee owned — If they don't have buy-in, you might as well opt out. Employees must take responsibility for their plans and generate the commitment and energy required to implement them. Ownership skyrockets when a plan is personalized to the individual, focused and specific, and doable in light of other activities.

Aligned with the employee's goals — Linking the plan to short-term and long-term goals tests whether activities are worth the effort they will take. When the going gets tough, this overt link can sustain focus and energy forward and toward one's bigger career objectives.

Linked to the needs of the organization — Let's get real. Resources are in short supply and support can be fickle. Both can be pulled at any time. Don't jeopardize your development efforts. If what employees are doing to learn and develop directly contributes to the bigger picture, you are on safe and solid ground.

DEBRIEF THE DEAL

Development activity is only that—activity—until it is properly unpacked to reveal its lessons. In fact, many employees become so engaged in the experience that they don't take the time to reflect on how they've benefitted from it. Yet again, conversation becomes the key to genuine growth, and simple questions help you launch dialogue that unpacks learning.

► What did you learn from that?

► In what ways were you challenged or stretched?

► What pitfalls or obstacles did you discover?

► Why were you successful? Or not?

► What would you do differently?

► What did you discover about yourself in the process?

► What guidelines or principles did you derive?

► How can you use your learning/insight in the future?

► How can you use your learning/insight in other contexts?

► What will you take away from this?

Just one or two of these questions can guide employees toward extracting learning from the experience.

In the process you'll seal the deal on their learning and development. But keep in mind that this sort of debriefing isn't the exclusive domain of the manager. Peers can help unpack learning among themselves and hold each other accountable. Alternately, skip-level conversations can be powerful, allowing employees to meet, get to know, and gain insights from your manager.

In fact, someone on your team may be looking to develop the ability to help others grow, speak the truth, or challenge others. Wouldn't debriefing another team member's learning be a great development

A few minutes of **conversation** can help others slow down enough to reflect, bring deep insights to the surface, **verbalize** important messages, and consider how to **leverage** their expanding skills and knowledge base.

experience for them? Remember, development opportunities are ever present and limited only by your own imagination.

Powerful possibilities emerge from the hindsight, foresight, and insight conversations you have with employees. But if you identify possibilities and insight and then fail to implement them, engagement and job satisfaction are likely to fall lower than if these possibilities were never identified at all.

This negative result is completely unnecessary because managers have three powerful ways to translate abstract inklings into tangible developmental action: through education, exposure, and experience.

What IF...

▶ everyone at every level consciously looked for what they could learn from others as well as what they could teach others?

▶ managers and employees were jointly committed to translating development ideas into action?

▶ development activities were considered incomplete until employees had a chance to reflect on and discuss what was learned?

9

Grow

with the **FLOW**

For me, it doesn't have to be a big sit-down meeting. In fact, I'd rather it wasn't. Doesn't it seem odd that something as important and personal as someone's career is put on an annual schedule... sort of like a termite inspection?

—An employee (perhaps yours)

Want real results? Take career development off the calendar and bring it into real everyday life.

We understand the reality. Many organizations feel the need for individual development planning (IDP) schedules and processes to ensure that career conversations happen. For some employees, it's the only way a development dialogue might ever occur. Although our research indicates that even with those processes in place, nearly 20 percent of those polled still don't get the "annual inspection."

But, as many businesses are abandoning event-based performance management processes for more frequent and ongoing interactions, it's only natural for career development to follow.

Don't get us wrong—we're all for the regular, planned career conversations—but on their own, they just don't cut it.

SUPPLEMENT THE SCHEDULED WITH THE SPONTANEOUS

What's needed is a more contemporary, organic, and effective way to supplement the scheduled with the spontaneous—to build development into the eternally evolving fabric of the workplace.

Consider the differences between these approaches:

Old Way	vs.	New Way
Taking it all off-line for the annual career discussion (that may be eleven months and three weeks away).		Operating real-time: Imagine connecting with employees in the instant, when something has just occurred or has been shared, in that moment of greatest receptivity when emotions (positive or negative) are fresh and people are open to deeper connections and insights.
An artificial conversation scheduled that you and the employee know is mandated by the organization in which you refer to a file of notes that might or might not make sense (since you took them up to eleven months and three weeks ago).		An authentic interaction: Imagine a genuine conversation, based on real and immediate stimulus within the workplace.
A batched approach to addressing career issues, where thirsty people are expected to drink from a fire hose and make it last another year.		An iterative approach: Imagine a layered approach, where information unfolds in digestible chunks, where awareness and insight are built bit by bit over time, where plans are incremental and employees can confidently develop, step by doable step.

Call it what you will: In the moment. On the spot. Context-sensitive. Instant. Bite-size. On the fly. Impromptu. Nano-coaching. Stealth development. We call it growing with the flow—workflow, that is.

> **"**I learned years ago that career development happens on its own schedule. The annual meeting is nice...but I use it more as a chance to summarize and capture highlights. I try to position myself to be there to support others throughout the year when real development—or the chance for it—occurs.**"**
>
> —Small business banker

DROP IN FOR DEVELOPMENT

Growing with the flow means development isn't limited to scheduled meetings; it becomes less burdensome in many ways. It can be quick— as short as one or two minutes. It can be casual—right on the shop floor or hanging over a cubicle wall. It can be completely unplanned—no notes or agendas to contend with. Hardly sounds like work, right?

But in life, there are always tradeoffs. When you grow with the flow, you save time and there is less planning involved. But you've got to be willing to give something as well. And that something in this case is a little more of your attention.

This approach places a new and non-negotiable demand upon managers. It requires that you drop in and heighten your sensitivity to the cues around you. It requires being present and in the moment. It requires noticing and acting upon opportunities as they arise.

Yet, when you think about it, being cue-sensitive is nothing more than a variation on the theme of curiosity.

Cue sensitivity is curiosity in action.

If you're cultivating curiosity in your conversations, it's not a huge leap to bring curiosity to the world around you. To pick up on what's going on under the surface. To look at situations and events with an eye toward "What can we learn from this?" To see the world around you as fodder for development.

CATCH A CUE

Sometimes you can learn more about a concept by studying it from an unusual angle. Along those lines, we've surveyed thousands of individuals across industries and asked them to share examples of times when their managers *missed* important career conversation cues. Which cues from the following list do you think might have come up in our results?

▶ The employee expresses an interest in learning something new

▶ Job responsibilities or expectations change

▶ The employee shares a concern or lack of confidence

▶ New project launches

▶ Old project ends

▶ Uncertain times in the industry or organization

▶ The employee takes on a new opportunity or assignment

▶ The employee is passed over for an opportunity or assignment

▶ New credentials or awards are earned

▶ The employee inquires about an opportunity

▶ A high-profile failure occurs

▶ Low-profile errors are made

▶ The employee demonstrates extra effort or interest

▶ Lack of effort or interest is noticed

▶ The employee shares something interesting they've read, seen, or heard

► Milestones are met

► Milestones are missed

► The employee appears to be struggling

► Things are going poorly

► Things are going well

Spoiler alert: Don't read further until you've made your guesses. We didn't trick you. Real employees—from various roles, levels, and industries—shared every one of these missed opportunities for development.

WHAT ABOUT YOU? ·

Review the list again and mark any (it's your book, go ahead, you won't get in trouble) that happened to you over the past week— opportunities for your manager to initiate a career conversation. Then ask yourself which of these might have occurred with your own employees over the past week. How many of these cues did you follow up on with a conversation?

Cues to grow with the flow abound—whether things are going well or poorly. People are hitting or missing deadlines. Winning or losing. The opportunities to leverage real life for real development are there—if we just develop the habit of looking for them.

PROMOTE A PAUSE

If recognizing a cue is the first step, then what's step two? Cause a pause. Just like tapping the pause button on any electronic device, briefly suspend the action so you can take advantage of the opportunity.

Pausing can redirect the momentum of the moment toward supporting and informing career growth.

Growing with the flow by having unplanned—but still intentional— conversations honors the cadence of business and the authentic, real-time, iterative nature of development. When you spot the cues and cause a pause, you encourage growth not just once a year but day in and day out.

FOCUS YOUR FLOW

Growing with the flow is nothing more than a conversation using the questions and approaches sprinkled throughout this book. You have everything you need to seize the moment and turn an opening into a development opportunity.

Pick a question—any question—that lets you delve into hindsight, foresight, or insight.

If the employee is struggling with a project, help look backward at strengths that contributed to the effort and what additional skills might be required. (Hindsight)

> **❝** It's counterintuitive, but when things aren't going well, that is the best time to focus on strengths. It gives the employee a needed boost and nearly always surfaces something they can tap into to help the situation.**❞**
>
> —Scientist/principal investigator

If the employee shares a story from the news about a competitor, explore what that means for the industry and your own organization. (Foresight)

> **❝** It's easy to get sucked into the day-to-day grind. I've got to find every opportunity possible to keep my crew thinking big picture. It helps the hotel and it helps them as individuals.**❞**
>
> —Hospitality team leader

If the employee has completed an assignment that was a stretch, open a conversation about the challenges encountered, what was learned, and how it can be applied. (Insight)

Ask a hindsight, foresight, or insight question and you'll have gone a long way toward seizing the moment and infusing career development into daily life. Ask the three questions together, and you have an unbeatable combination.

When you make it a habit to help others grow with the flow, additional benefits follow. Your regularly scheduled career conversations will be richer and more efficient because of the effort you've invested throughout the year. And over time, you'll train employees to pick up on their own cues, cause their own pauses, and take greater ownership for driving their own development. The benefits of this kind of growing just keep flowing.

What IF . . .

► employees felt like their careers were precious gems to be polished frequently over time?

► you were in the habit of leveraging day-to-day life at work toward development?

► annual career conversations were the culmination of growing with the flow throughout the year?

Culture
Shift

The organization says it's all about supporting my career development…but only if it's convenient and fits into their tidy process.

—An employee (perhaps yours)

What individual managers do matters. A lot. Their intentions, relationships, and interactions contribute to a tone within the organization. And they can change the lives of those who work for them.

Being heard. Being recognized. Being valued. Being trusted. Being developed. This resonates deeply with employees. And this is what happens when managers commit to a regular cadence of career conversations.

Yet, if one manager's efforts can have such an influence at the individual level, imagine the effect of a constructive organizational culture on your workforce as a whole.

Culture counts when it comes to **career development**.

When culture aligns with and supports development, it creates a synergist tsunami, sweeping layers of leadership, policies and practices, and fundamental sensibilities up and washing them all over the organization. Stragglers can't hold out for long. They either join in or choose to go elsewhere.

And, in the process, the organization as a whole reaps the benefits of highly effective career development. Engagement. Customer satisfaction. Discretionary effort. Sales. Innovation. Retention. Quality. Productivity. Reputation. Loyalty. Profitability.

Cultures that actively support career development and enjoy its constructive by-products might look very different on the outside. They can be for-profit or not-for-profit. They can be product or service oriented. They can be large or small. High-tech or low-tech. Private or public. But, under the veneer, these organizations share five fundamental characteristics or cultural markers.

How does your organization stack up? Complete this short survey to assess where things currently stand—and how you can be part of a cultural revolution to enhance support for authentic, sustainable career development. (Go ahead and write in the book. It's yours. In any case, you can get a clean, expanded version of this survey at www.Help -Them-Grow.com.)

CULTIVATE A CAREER DEVELOPMENT CULTURE

This assessment and model are adapted from the work of
DesignArounds, 2017.

	Disagree				Agree
Trust levels are high enough for people to routinely tell the truth and be candid.	1	2	3	4	5
Honest, helpful information about organizational and individual performance, business strategies, and future opportunities is easily accessible throughout the organization.	1	2	3	4	5
Total: Information-Rich					
Questions and the open exchange of ideas are actively encouraged by executives, leaders, and employees alike.	1	2	3	4	5
Risk-taking and experimentation are rewarded and celebrated.	1	2	3	4	5
Total: Curious					
Development is valued as an ongoing investment over time, not as a once-and-done activity.	1	2	3	4	5
It's generally acknowledged that people develop at different speeds and in a variety of ways.	1	2	3	4	5
Total: Patient (with the Development Process)					
Managers give employees appropriate levels of authority to make decisions about how the work gets done.	1	2	3	4	5
Organizational structures can easily morph in response to changing business needs.	1	2	3	4	5
Total: Results-Focused					
Us and them is not part of the lexicon or anyone's thinking.	1	2	3	4	5
People are encouraged to look outside of their own areas for opportunities to learn, contribute, and grow.	1	2	3	4	5
Total: Blurry around Boundaries					

What do you think? How is your organization doing?

► Scores of 8–10 in any category suggest that this cultural characteristic is alive and well and actively supporting career development.

► Scores of 6–8 in any category indicate that while this characteristic is present at least some of the time, it might not be strong enough to create the cultural web of support required to get the most from career development.

► Scores of 5 or below in any category highlight an area where the culture might be out of step with what's required to enable the kind of development employees expect and that the organization needs.

What does it all mean? More important, what can you do to contribute to a culture shift within your organization? Read on.

INFORMATION-RICH

Career development flourishes in an environment of openness and transparency. Information flows freely. Which is essential because information about performance, perceptions, and possibilities is precisely what employees need to own their development and to drive it forward. That means the job requirements, competencies, and ways to develop them are accessible to everyone. That means that managers and leaders at all levels make feedback and coaching a top priority. That means that employees are never left wondering about how they're currently doing or what steps they need to take to grow. When this happens, trust inspires an upward spiral of truth-telling and information sharing.

► **TRY THIS**

· ·

Do you want to cultivate greater information richness within your organization?

► Demonstrate candor and tell the truth; and recognize others who do the same.

► Generously share information about the organization's strategy and plans.

► Practice open-book management and make financial data available to all employees.

► Make foresight an ongoing conversation to ensure that everyone understands the big picture.

► Offer feedback and coaching to others—and demonstrate what it looks like to receive it as well.

CURIOSITY

Just as curiosity fuels an effective career conversation, it also fuels a development-supportive culture. You see it when leaders bring genuine inquisitiveness to their interactions with others. Or when "seeking out diverse points of view" is not a talking point but instead the whole point of dialogue. Or when those deemed as troublemakers in other organizations—the people who have a reputation for asking *why* and *why not*—aren't marginalized but are instead well regarded in the organization. Or when people are routinely encouraged to take risks...and are not punished when experiments don't play out exactly as planned.

▶ **TRY THIS**

. . . .

Want to cultivate greater curiosity within your organization?

▶ Shift your conversational cadence to include more questions and fewer statements.

▶ Actively—and visibly—seek out contrarians and welcome devil's advocates.

▶ Challenge yourself to look at people and situations with fresh eyes.

▶ Celebrate smart risks run afoul and dispassionately debrief them with the spirit of discovery.

▶ Dramatically expand your repertoire of possibility questions such as *What if?, How might it work?,* and *How can we?*

PATIENT (WITH THE DEVELOPMENT PROCESS)

In today's environment, where results are monitored by the hour and *long term* means next week, patience is in short supply. But managers and leaders who make career development a reality rather than a rallying slogan appreciate the value in focusing on a slightly longer horizon. They don't need to wrap things up immediately. Rather, they allow thoughts, ideas, and opportunities to evolve organically over time. They appreciate that everyone grows at their own rate and in their own way and flex accordingly. Flexibility, commitment, and consistency are the hallmarks of this cultural characteristic.

▶ **TRY THIS**

. . . .

Want to cultivate greater patience with the development process within your organization?

▶ Challenge yourself and others to balance long-term development goals with more short-term, pressing business needs.

- ▶ Welcome mistakes and failures as valuable steps in the learning process.

- ▶ Take a "time-released" approach to development, making small, ongoing investments in others over time versus dispensing a massive occasional dose.

- ▶ Give people the space to attain their comfortable level of competence before pressing them forward.

- ▶ Set aside, prioritize, and protect the funds required for development...every single fiscal period.

RESULTS-ORIENTED

Development is a big-picture game. What are we trying to achieve? What are our goals? Focusing broadly on results—and being less rigid (within reason) about how they are accomplished—provides a wide berth within which employees can experiment, try out new talents and skills, approach tasks differently, and grow their capacity. Leadership clarity about the *what* can allow for more creativity and flexibility around the *how*, creating countless vehicles for growth.

▶ TRY THIS

Do you want to cultivate a greater results orientation within your organization?

- ▶ Routinely ask employees how best to achieve organizational goals—and then give them the authority and autonomy to run with viable ideas.

- ▶ Actively engage those closest to the work in developing new procedures, systems, and tools to improve the process.

- ▶ Celebrate and promote examples of employee initiative and innovation.

▶ Be open to experimenting with different structures and approaches...just as long as they are designed to deliver necessary results.

BLURRY AROUND BOUNDARIES

Cultures that support career development tend to have leaders with very blurry vision. In this case, though, blurry vision doesn't require a doctor's visit; on the contrary, it's quite healthy. Rather than seeing hard lines between departments or divisions, these leaders see opportunities to collaborate. Instead of *us* and *them*, they see how *all of us* are in this together. Rather than looking out for themselves, these leaders look out for the enterprise. They actively encourage development because they can look outside of their own areas for opportunities for their people to learn, contribute, and grow. They're willing to move people around and even lose good talent to their colleagues as a way to support the development of employees. And in the process, these sorts of leaders build an unbeatable reputation, culture, and organization.

▶ TRY THIS
. . . .

Want to cultivate blurrier boundaries within your organization?

▶ Get to know your colleagues in other areas of the business and learn about contributions to the organization and the challenges they face.

▶ Demonstrate respect for other leaders in all you say and do.

▶ Expose employees to other parts of the organization as much and as frequently as possible.

▶ Squash even hints of territorialism and competition with other departments before they take hold.

▶ Seek out collaboration with colleagues that offer development experiences for your staff.

Organizations that reflect these characteristics are serious about career development. And, just as careers develop one conversation at a time over time, cultures develop over time through the consistent commitment of individual developmentally minded managers. This is clearly something organizations need and employees want.

What IF? . . .

▶ Everyone at every level was held accountable for career development?

▶ Talent was really treated like an enterprise-wide resource?

▶ Career development was tracked and reported right alongside other important business metrics?

▶ Development became your organization's secret weapon for attracting and retaining top talent?

CONCLUSION

THE DEVELOPMENT DIFFERENCE

Helping employees grow is an essential management responsibility. But for you, it's likely a lot more than that. You didn't go into supervision because you love the scheduling, performance appraisals, and other administrative duties. You did it because of your own career aspirations and development and because you wanted to make a difference in the organization and in those who report to you.

There are lots of ways to make a difference.

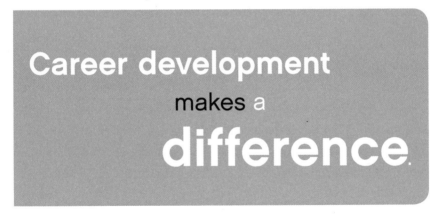

Career development makes a **difference**.

Just talk with people. In today's workplace, everyone knows that employees own their careers. But there's a lot you can do through conversation to help focus, energize, and activate that ownership toward satisfying results by merely talking with employees. **Interact intentionally.**

Keep learning about employees—and help them learn about themselves—throughout their careers. Genuine interest is too frequently in short supply, yet it goes a long way toward building loyalty, retention, and results. Using hindsight as a lens to understand who employees are and what they bring to the party in terms of skills, interests, values, and more will provide a solid foundation for development. **Keep the interview going.**

Encourage and enable foresight. What people are good at, what they love, and how they like to work needs to be filtered through a foresight lens. When you help employees develop the ability to scan the environment, anticipate trends, and spot opportunities, you provide a constructive context for career development. **Foster a future focus.**

Leverage the insights that come from hindsight and foresight conversations. Help others see where their hindsight and foresight overlap. Opportunities exist where what the employee wants to do can find expression in the real, ever-changing world of work. **Mine the intersection of hindsight and foresight for insight.**

Paint a more expansive picture of career development and available growth opportunities. Most people have blinders on when it comes to how to advance their careers, and they look only upward. Internalize and promote the climbing wall concept. **Develop in all directions.**

Help people focus on what they want to do versus what they want to be. Title- and role-based development is inherently limiting. No opening...no development. But if you can help employees tease out what they want to do, you can help them move beyond the need to move. **Elevate development in place to its rightful place.**

Support others as they think through how to turn their career goals into action. Ideas and objectives are a good starting point, but they don't get far without the creativity of opportunity mindedness, the tactical focus of planning, and the ongoing conversations that help employees recognize and make the most of education, exposure, and experiences designed for development. **Support the process.**

Find ways to bring development to life day in and day out. Waiting for an annual or prescheduled meeting to discuss career matters robs you and the employee of the energy and opportunities that are present always

CAREER DEVELOPMENT

is one of the most **powerful** and underutilized **levers** managers have to **drive** engagement, retention, and **results**.

and everywhere. Infuse development conversations into the workflow and see how quickly they permeate the culture. **Grow with the flow.**

Contribute to the culture. Help to create an environment that supports this kind of authentic and sustainable development. Talk with other managers about the key characteristics. Challenge and hold each other accountable—for your employees and the organization. **Make a culture shift.**

The reason we all love levers is because their sole purpose is to produce the magic of big results from proportionately smaller forces. If you're wondering where to start, it doesn't matter: doing something—*anything*—has significant power. Start small. Start anywhere.

Pick one of the following actions.

► Dedicate the next month to delving into hindsight with one or two employees.

► Schedule a foresight forum with your group.

► Share the idea of the career-climbing wall at a team meeting and get reaction.

► Put the Development Dictionary page 87 from this book in front of an employee and use it to discuss opportunities.

► Watch for cues to engage in short, spontaneous development discussions.

► Apply all of this to your next IDP.

What IF . . .

► you put just one or two ideas into practice with employees right now?

They would **grow**—
the business would **grow**—
and so would **you**.

ACKNOWLEDGMENTS

This second edition would not have been possible without the thousands of readers who appreciated the value of career development and took a chance on *Help Them Grow or Watch Them Go*. Your feedback and insights have deepened our understanding of the topic and the evolving workplace within which development only becomes more critical.

The same goes for our clients who allowed us the privilege of sharing these ideas throughout their organizations. Each consulting engagement, keynote presentation, and training session challenged us to consider the concepts and their application in new and different ways. We are grateful for your confidence and collaboration.

Sincere thanks go to the thousands of managers and employee we've had the opportunity to cross paths with over the years. Your experiences, candor, and wisdom fill each page of this book as they've filled our hearts over the years.

And we can't forget about the foreign publishers who have made *Help Them Grow or Watch Them Go* available to Spanish-, Portuguese-, Mandarin-, Russian-, and Farsi-speaking readers. Thank you for helping to spread these ideas, supporting development globally, and facilitating connections that make the world feel a bit smaller and warmer to both of us.

We continue to deeply appreciate the "originals"—the team of colleagues and friends who contributed to the first edition. Ann Jordan from Career Systems International (now part of Talent Dimensions) lent her years of career development expertise, creative energy, and expansive thinking to the effort. Karen Voloshin from DesignArounds was there from the very beginning, offering content, positioning, and her innate understanding of and focus on the manager. Lindsay Watkins, Lorianne Speaks, and Liz Price were (and continue to be) invaluable partners. Jennifer Papineau built upon the original look and feel so skillfully crafted by Nancy Austin with additional graphics in this second edition. And we're more grateful than ever for our mutual friend, Judy Estrin, who brought us together in the first place.

None of this would have been possible without the urging and support of Steve Piersanti and the publishing team at Berrett-Koehler. When we write about exceptional managers, Steve is our model. His authentic, straightforward, generous, curious, and humble style of leadership inspires those around him and sparks remarkable development and results. We're grateful to have been led by Steve. And Berrett-Koehler extended to this new edition the same love, attention, and support that its predecessor received.

We're most grateful to those closest to us who have helped us grow over the years. Team Giulioni has been in Julie's corner from the start. Peter, Jenna, Nick, and Diane have spent hours listening to half-baked ideas, sharing their experiences, and only rolling their eyes occasionally. Karen Voloshin partnered with Julie and DesignArounds clients, always inventing new and more effective learning approaches. And Laurie Chatham provided the ideal writer's retreat.

Team Kaye was equally supportive. Career Systems International associates, who presented the work worldwide, helped refine the message and brought specific feedback from the audiences they delivered to. Cile Johnson and Lynn Cowart, who lead these teams generously, offered their time and attention to Bev in support of this initiative. And of course, Barry, Lindsey, and Jill rooted for Bev whenever the going got tough. Barry accommodated Bev's scribbles in the middle of the night, and Roxy was there for support each step of the way.

And finally, we acknowledge each other—two very different individuals with one very similar focus on development. Working together on both editions has helped us grow—so now we'll let you go.

INDEX

ABOUT THE AUTHORS

PHOTO: MICHAEL NEWAN PHOTOGRAPHY

The authors Julie Winkle Giulioni (left) and Beverly Kaye (right).

DR. BEVERLY KAYE

Dr. Beverly Kaye is recognized internationally as a professional dedicated to helping individuals, managers, and organizations understand the practical how-to principles of employee development, engagement, and retention. Her books and learning materials have stood the test of time. ATD (the Association for Talent Development) honored her with their 2018 Lifetime Achievement Award, and ISA (the Association of Learning Professionals) honored her with their 2018 Thought Leadership Award for her body of work.

Beverly's contributions to the field of career development have been used by talent professionals for decades. She foresaw the effects of leaner and flatter organizations on individual careers and described a systems approach to building a development culture. She became an early game changer in an area of practice that heretofore had only been partially explored. *Up Is Not the Only Way* (2017) looked at career mobility and delivered an action-packed guidebook for employees and managers. It highlighted the career choices that were available other than the traditional ladder. Her work in engagement and retention continued a commitment to offering practical strategies for today's workforce. The message in *Love 'Em or Lose 'Em* (2014) and its companion *Love It, Don't Leave It* (2003) has been delivered to companies worldwide. *Hello Stay Interviews, Goodbye Talent Loss* (2015) was designed for managers who want to stem the tide of exit interviews.

Beverly founded Career Systems International and recently transitioned its ownership and legacy to key members of her leadership team. She supports the rebranded enterprise, Talent Dimensions, who deliver and expertly expand on her thought leadership. Bev is a Jersey Girl living in Sherman Oaks, California. She's been married for forty-five years to her ex–rocket scientist husband, Barry, and is mom to a grown-up daughter, Lindsey, and a grown-up dog, Roxy.

JULIE WINKLE GIULIONI

Julie Winkle Giulioni and her firm DesignArounds create award-winning performance improvement solutions that enhance employee development, engagement, retention, and the bottom line. Named one of *Inc. Magazine*'s top-100 speakers, Julie has traveled from Russia to China to Lithuania and beyond, helping leaders around the world help others grow. She's a sought-after speaker for consistently delivering creative insights as well as practical takeaways that change behavior.

Prior to founding DesignArounds, Julie led product development at AchieveGlobal. Managing cross-functional and international teams of marketing, creative, instructional design, and production profession-als, she directed the creation and launch of products that are used in tens of thousands of organizations globally. Before that, Julie held mul-tiple training management positions and was a professor and depart-ment chair at Woodbury University. She is a regular contributor to *The Economist, The Conference Board, SmartBrief,* and other publications. Industry awards and recognition include *Human Resource Executive Magazine*'s Top Ten Training Products, a Global HR Excellence Award from the World HR Congress, New York Film Festival, and Lguide rec-ognition for developing "e-learning at its best."

When Julie is not working with clients, she's active in her commu-nity. A Southern California native, she's as comfortable doing stand-up paddle boarding as she is doing stand-up training. She currently lives with her husband, Peter, and their pooch Pixel, in South Pasadena.

WORKING WITH THE AUTHORS

Bev and Julie each have their own independent companies that offer an array of specialized products and services. They came together to create this powerful book on developing talent through career conversations, and they partner often in their separate consulting practices. Both deliver exceptional keynote speeches globally and have their own websites in addition to www.Help-Them-Grow.com.

BEV KAYE & CO.

Beverly Kaye founded Career Systems International (now part of Talent Dimensions) more than three decades ago to offer innovative ways to help organizations solve their greatest talent challenges by engaging, developing, and retaining their people. Bev Kaye & Co., in conjunction with Talent Dimensions, provides a comprehensive portfolio of award-winning learning solutions and services globally to a broad base of industries and organizations, including nearly two-thirds of the Fortune 1000 companies.

Conversations are the common thread and outcome for all of our areas of expertise. Simple, but powerful, these critical conversations

Our unique approach to organizational learning has always demanded solutions that are deceptively simple, delightfully engaging, deliberately flexible, and decidedly business-centric. These principles always guide us in developing and delivering solutions that provide high impact and measurable results.

around engaging, growing, mentoring, and retaining talent ignite vital connections between employees, managers, and their organizations. Clients consistently report that they get powerful results as they create a strong voice for all their people in a surround-sound world.

Improving the business performance of our clients and the lives of all employees who seek to maximize their personal and professional potential is key to our offerings.

PRACTICAL SOLUTIONS

Career development. Career development consistently ranks as a top driver in employee engagement, not only impacting retention but also fueling an organization with innovative, productive, and impassioned employees. The CareerPower suite teaches employees to self-power their careers and teaches managers to act as a sounding board and career coach to drive the learning and growth of the individuals on their team. We offer webinars and learning solutions to support *Help Them Grow*. These solutions, offered in a variety of delivery methods, are highly interactive and provide assessments, tools, and activities to have managers and employees return to the job with actionable plans, the skill, and the confidence to hold meaningful development conversations.

Engaging and retaining talent. Engaging people and impacting business results requires managers to have a unique set of skills to effectively influence employee commitment. The learning solutions that support *Love 'Em or Lose 'Em: Getting Good People to Stay* provide today's leaders with the experience, knowledge, communication, and confidence to drive engagement worldwide. Though managers play a crucial role, employees can also take charge of their own satisfaction. *Love It, Don't Leave It* empowers individuals to create the conditions they need to improve job satisfaction without having to leave. As managers use the "Stay Interviews" and employees become comfortable in their roles, engagement truly becomes a two-way street, and business results are maximized.

Consulting support. Our consultant team understands the importance of providing a strategic perspective to maximize business results for all of our solutions. We work to focus on an organization's culture, resource requirements, human resource structures, long-range goals, and business plans. The more our learning solutions are embedded in the larger system, the more impactful they can be.

Bev Kaye & Co., www.BevKaye.com, 818-995-6454
Talent Dimensions, www.Talent-Dimensions.com, 800-577-6916

DESIGNAROUNDS

Julie Winkle Giulioni and her partner, Karen Voloshin, are cofounders and principals of DesignArounds, a bicoastal learning and development firm committed to maximizing individual and organizational potential through customized learning experiences. Although their work spans the full range of leadership topics, Julie and Karen have a passion for bringing *Help Them Grow or Watch Them Go* concepts to life in organizations around the globe. DesignArounds's custom-designed learning experiences based on this best-selling book are the natural next step for leaders and employees who want to reconceive development in today's evolving workplace, build development into the daily workflow, and acquire the new skills required to engage in meaningful conversation and planning to support ongoing growth.

DesignArounds matches just the right format with the needs of organizations and learners. Choices include custom

▶ keynote speeches

▶ instructor-led workshops

▶ webinars

We are passionate about bringing together the needs of learners, desired organizational outcomes, and effective learning methods to produce powerful results. With DesignArounds, you can count on us for solutions that are always engaging, relevant, actionable... and designed around you.

► coaching

► e-learning

► microlearning

Train-the-trainer certifications allow internal facilitators to share the message within your organization; and Julie, Karen, and other highly skilled DesignArounds facilitators are also available to deliver high-impact workshops and webinars. But that's just the start of the journey. Embedding a development mindset and skill set in an organization requires a systems approach. The centerpiece of the Design-Arounds system is the flexible e-Grow platform, filled with a tailored selection of content-rich, bite-size audio, video, text, and activity-based resources that turn new skills into long-term habits. Accessed on-demand, e-Grow offers learners the tools they want, when they want them to extend expertise, boost confidence, and realize results.

Julie Winkle Giulioni, www.juliewinklegiulioni.com, 626-799-3418
Karen Voloshin, www.designarounds.com, 203-393-2261

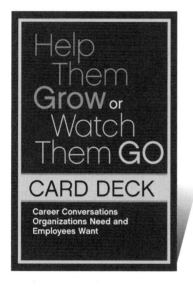

Other Books Coauthored by Beverly Kaye
Up Is Not the Only Way
Rethinking Career Mobility

Move up or move out. When those two options appear to be the only ones, dissatisfaction grows and engagement suffers. In decades of studying careers around the globe, Beverly Kaye, Lindy Williams, and Lynn Cowart have found that, in fact, there are more options. And rethinking career mobility can lead you to them!

The authors show how managers, coaches, and employees can partner to determine what's best and what's next. Keep the same job but discover new ways to learn and grow? Explore moving to a position that could be a better fit? Step back without getting derailed? This book encourages readers to take a "kaleidoscope" view—to be open to ever-shifting patterns of opportunities and possibilities—so they can create a unique, personalized path to a truly rewarding career.

Paperback, 152 pages, 978-1-5230-8348-0
PDF ebook 978-1-5230-8349-7
ePub ebook 978-1-5230-8350-3
Digital Audio 978-1-5230-8352-7

BK Berrett–Koehler Publishers, Inc.
www.bkconnection.com   800.929.2929

Love 'Em or Lose 'Em, 5th ed.
Getting Good People to Stay

26 research-based strategies—from A to Z—for engaging and retaining employees

A *Wall Street Journal* Bestseller

Whether you manage talented people in a large or small organization—in Dublin, Denver, Dalian, or Dubai—you have a common goal with managers anywhere in the world. You want to hang on to your stars—your high performers and solid citizens alike.

And we don't mean desperately cling to them. We mean fully engage them! Have them pumped up, excited to come to work for you every day, and willing to bring their discretionary effort with them.

How will you do that? This book will be your guide.

Paperback, 328 pages, 978-1-60994-884-9
PDF ebook 978-1-60994-885-6
ePub ebook 978-1-60994-886-3
CD/Audio 978-1-57675-120-6

BK® Berrett–Koehler Publishers, Inc.
www.bkconnection.com

800.929.2929

Hello Stay Interviews, Goodbye Talent Loss

A Manager's Playbook

Stay interviews prevent exit interviews!

Worried that your talented people will want things you can't deliver, like more money or a big promotion? Beverly Kaye and Sharon Jordan-Evans have a simple four-step process for dealing with that. Not sure how to get started? They provide dozens of suggested questions and icebreakers. Think you don't have time? They offer all kinds of creative time-saving options for where, when, and how you can do stay interviews.

Paperback, 120 pages, 978-1-62656-347-6
PDF ebook 978-1-62656-348-3
ePub ebook 978-1-62656-349-0
Digital Audio 978-1-62656-650-7

Love It, Don't Leave It!
26 Ways to Get What You Want at Work

Love It, Don't Leave It provides readers with 26 ways to make their current work environment more satisfying. Presented in an appealing, accessible A-to-Z format, *Love It, Don't Leave It* includes strategies for improving communication, stimulating career growth, balancing work with family, and much more. Designed for workers at any age and at any stage, *Love It, Don't Leave It* helps people assume responsibility for the way their work lives work. Readers who try just a few of the strategies in this book may find that the job they want is the job they already have.

Paperback, 216 pages, 978-1-57675-250-0
PDF ebook 978-1-57675-875-5
ePub ebook 978-1-60994-364-6

Berrett–Koehler Publishers, Inc.
www.bkconnection.com

800.929.2929

Berrett–Koehler
Publishers

Berrett-Koehler is an independent publisher dedicated to an ambitious mission: Connecting people and ideas to create a world that works for all.

We believe that the solutions to the world's problems will come from all of us, working at all levels: in our organizations, in our society, and in our own lives. Our BK Business books help people make their organizations more humane, democratic, diverse, and effective (we don't think there's any contradiction there). Our BK Currents books offer pathways to creating a more just, equitable, and sustainable society. Our BK Life books help people create positive change in their lives and align their personal practices with their aspirations for a better world.

All of our books are designed to bring people seeking positive change together around the ideas that empower them to see and shape the world in a new way.

And we strive to practice what we preach. At the core of our approach is Stewardship, a deep sense of responsibility to administer the company for the benefit of all of our stakeholder groups including authors, customers, employees, investors, service providers, and the communities and environment around us. Everything we do is built around this and our other key values of quality, partnership, inclusion, and sustainability.

This is why we are both a B-Corporation and a California Benefit Corporation—a certification and a for-profit legal status that require us to adhere to the highest standards for corporate, social, and environmental performance.

We are grateful to our readers, authors, and other friends of the company who consider themselves to be part of the BK Community. We hope that you, too, will join us in our mission.

A BK Business Book

We hope you enjoy this BK Business book. BK Business books pioneer new leadership and management practices and socially responsible approaches to business. They are designed to provide you with groundbreaking and practical tools to transform your work and organizations while upholding the triple bottom line of people, planet, and profits. High-five!

To find out more, visit **www.bkconnection.com**.

Berrett–Koehler
Publishers

Connecting people and ideas
to create a world that works for all

Dear Reader,

Thank you for picking up this book and joining our worldwide community of Berrett-Koehler readers. We share ideas that bring positive change into people's lives, organizations, and society.

To welcome you, we'd like to offer you a free e-book. You can pick from among twelve of our bestselling books by entering the promotional code **BKP92E** here: http://www.bkconnection.com/welcome.

When you claim your free e-book, we'll also send you a copy of our e-news-letter, the *BK Communiqué*. Although you're free to unsubscribe, there are many benefits to sticking around. In every issue of our newsletter you'll find

- A free e-book
- Tips from famous authors
- Discounts on spotlight titles
- Hilarious insider publishing news
- A chance to win a prize for answering a riddle

Best of all, our readers tell us, "Your newsletter is the only one I actually read." So claim your gift today, and please stay in touch!

Sincerely,

Charlotte Ashlock
Steward of the BK Website

Questions? Comments? Contact me at bkcommunity@bkpub.com.

MIX
Paper from
responsible sources
FSC® C016245
www.fsc.org

Certified

Corporation
bcorporation.net